For Harry,
Whose advice made it
possible —

Claire C. Benton

Who Wants to Buy a Water Company?

from private to public control in New Haven

Who Wants to Buy a Water Company?

from private to public control in New Haven

Dorothy S. McCluskey and Claire C. Bennitt

Rutledge Books, Inc.

Bethel, CT

ALL RIGHTS RESERVED
Rutledge Books, Inc.
8 F.J. Clarke Circle, Bethel, CT 06801

Manufactured in the United States of America

Cataloging in Publication Data
McCluskey, Dorothy S.
Who wants to buy a water company?: from private to
public control in New Haven/Dorothy S. McCluskey and
Claire C. Bennitt
p. cm.
ISBN 1-887750-39-8
1. South Central Connecticut Regional Water
Authority. 2. Land use—Connecticut.
3. Water resources development—Connecticut. 4.
Public utilities—Connecticut. I. Bennitt, Claire C.
II. Title.
363.6—dc20   LC 96-71042
                                                              CIP

Contents

ILLUSTRATIONS

FRONTISPIECE

It is a matter for serious and farsighted study and fair-minded negotiation, by the ablest and broadest men who can be secured to represent the city and the water company, to devise a wise, just and businesslike permanent policy for the control and development of these lands and for governing the relations of the city and the company in regard to them. . . .

Considered merely as a source of water supply and looking many, many years into the future, the time would probably come when parts of this land would attain such value, and the whole of its water supply would have become so small a fraction of the total required for the city, that the value of the watershed for residential development might outweigh its value as a collecting reservoir.

It is inconceivable, however, judging from the experience of all large cities the world over, that its value to the public for purposes of recreation, when combined with that for water supply, would ever fall below its market value as private real estate.

Frederick Law Olmstead, Jr., and Cass Gilbert, *Report to the New Haven Civic Improvement Commission,* (New Haven: Tuttle, Morehouse and Taylor, 1910), 44.

PREFACE

Why Write a History of the Regional Water Authority?

Implicit in putting together a history, whether of a sleepy old water company or of a nation poised on the brink of revolutionary change, is the fact that a story is being told. This is a story of transforming a private investor-owned water utility into public ownership, of overcoming mutual urban and suburban mistrust to regionalize the company that delivers water—a natural resource with no respect for political boundaries. It is a story of high finance and of political deals. It is a story of land use planning, of open space and recreation. Mostly, it is a story of people, and of how they solved real and perceived problems.

Originally conceived as a chronicle documenting how and why the regional authority came to be, this history evolved into a real world model of how a regional water utility can balance open space conservation and fiscal responsibility to consumers in an environmentally sound manner.

By publishing this book, we hope to help water utility managers, town planners, environmentalists, consumer advocates, and others to strike a similar balance in their own community or region. This can fulfill a need wherever the capital cost of improvements required by the Federal Safe Drinking Water Act of 1974 places water utility owned open space at risk of development, or whenever the sale of watershed land is perceived as a means of increasing a return to shareholders.

Connecticut may well be the first state to confront the water utility land sales debate. It certainly is not the last. Watershed protection and the need for drinking water filtration continue to be issues of national importance. Other states are observing Connecticut's experience with intense interest. Ownership of New York City's water system and management of its upstate watersheds is currently under negotiation.

The authors of this history were active participants, from concept to birth to maturity, in the transformation of the private water company into a public regional water authority.

A Connecticut State Representative from 1975 to 1982, Dorothy Soest McCluskey chaired the Environment Subcommittee on Sale of Water Company Land. She also has served as Project Manager of the Connecticut Inland Wetlands Project, a Ford Foundation Pilot Project, 1973-1974, and as Director of Government Relations for The Nature Conservancy Connecticut Chapter from 1985 to 1990.

She is a graduate of Wheaton College with a BA degree, and also received an MFS degree from Yale University School of Forestry and Environmental Studies in 1973 where she concentrated on environmental planning and water resource management. Mrs. McCluskey is the author of *Conservation Plan for North Branford*, 1970, and co-author of *Evaluation of Inland Wetland and Watercourse Functions*, 1974.

Claire Clark Bennitt, a resident of North Branford when the threat of massive land sales galvanized New Haven area communities into action, worked with Representative McCluskey in the state legislature as her Administrative Assistant. She represented Representative McCluskey at many Feasibility Study Commission meetings and was invited to serve as liason between this Commission and the state Council on Water Company Lands.

Appointed to the original South Central Connecticut Regional Water Authority in September, 1977, Ms. Bennitt served in that capacity throughout the efforts to regionalize the water utility. Elected as Secretary-Treasurer at the RWA's organizational meeting, she continues to hold that office.

She is a graduate of Wellesley College with a major in history.

PART ONE

Reasons for Going Public: Issues, An Overview

Introduction

The story begins with a very conservative old water utility called New Haven Water Company. Through masterful planning, the Water Company developed its extensive water supply system of reservoirs and well fields, water mains and pumping stations—all sufficient to serve over 400,000 people. It amassed more than 25,000 acres of land, most of it watershed, for its drinking water supply. After more than a hundred years, it was running efficiently and quietly, delivering high quality water to the city whose name it bore and to the suburbs growing up around it.

Accomplishing this feat had not been easy. Ever since the company was chartered in 1849, there had been debate over private versus city ownership. Finally, when several entrepreneurs successfully formed a private water company, they agreed on a contract with the City of New Haven that prevented the company from neglecting the public need in its pursuit of profit.[1] One of these entrepreneurs, Eli Whitney II, wrote in his diary that he constructed the water works with the expectation that he would someday sell it to the city.[2]

City efforts, in 1881 and 1891, to purchase the water works were unsuccessful, but did lead, in 1902, to a contract to settle their disagreements. The basic provisions of this contract called for free water for fire and schools and fair rates for city customers. However, it also gave New Haven a future purchase option once every twenty five years.[3] (see Appendix C)

Seventy years later this provision became the key instrument for unlocking the door to public ownership.

At that time, environmental concerns over the use of natural resources became the focus of national public debate and laws, including the Federal Safe Drinking Water Act of 1974. Connecticut took this mandate more seriously than many states and adopted regulations exceeding the federal requirements and leading to the filtration of surface water supplies. To raise sufficient capital to meet the new requirements, the Company announced it would sell vast acres of its open space land in the seventeen communities it served.

This land sale proposal became the catalyst for regional ownership. The stage was now set for public acquisition.

Would the City of New Haven, exercising its 1902 option to purchase the Water Company, win out? Would the political forces supporting continued private ownership have enough clout to provide desperately needed capital for a financially strapped business facing major construction to meet the requirements of the federal Safe Drinking Water Act of 1974? These questions were debated hotly.

The July 4, 1979 headline of New Haven's morning newspaper, *The Journal-Courier*, proclaimed "Accord reached for sale of Water Co." A year later, on August 26, 1980, the actual transfer of ownership from the private shareholders of the Water Company to the publicly owned South Central Connecticut Regional Water Authority took place, ending a decade long battle over the water utility's ownership and the management of its extensive land holdings.

Set against the backdrop of urban-suburban mistrust, proposed massive sales of "surplus" water company land, fledgling efforts at regionalization, constraints of federal and state mandates requiring filtration of drinking water supplies, and increased water rates, the story of public ownership of the Water Company becomes a fascinating voyage into the past.

Sale of Water Company Land: 1974-1979

On January 2, 1974, the Water Company announced its intent to sell over 16,000 acres of its 26,000 acres of land holdings in seventeen New Haven area towns. The announcement triggered a storm of opposition from the towns, state officials and private individuals. State Attorney General Robert K. Killian accused the company of "public-be-damned arrogance of a high order" and denounced Water Company President Charles E. Woods for his plan to sell off thousands of acres of irreplaceable water company open space land, charging that this plan would "return huge profits from the sale to utility company shareholders".[4] Financier and former state environmental commissioner Dan W. Lufkin vowed to fight against the land sales as a private citizen.[5]

Towns and the state had assumed water company land would remain open space. Sale and development of this watershed land were contrary to towns' plans of development and sewer facility programs and conflicted with the state Plan of Conservation and Development and with state Department of Health policy. Town officials feared the fiscal impact of private development and the accompanying need for municipal services and saw municipal purchase of the land as financially infeasible.

Although state law governing the sale of public service company land gave a town a first chance to buy the property, it provided only 180 days for the town to obtain financing. Even without this time constraint, the price of the land, most of it beautiful rolling land in rapidly growing suburban communities, was so high that few towns or even the state could afford to buy it. Assuming a conservative market value of $2,000 per acre, the total purchase cost would be $32,000,000.

Of New Haven Water Company land, only four acres were in New Haven, the rest in the surrounding towns with North Branford (5,723), Madison (4,325), Guilford (3,237) and Bethany (3,066) leading the list.

Sale of water company land was the most critical land use planning issue facing not only the greater New Haven area but the entire state. At stake was the future of 133,000 acres of Connecticut's countryside bought since the turn of the century by water utilities for

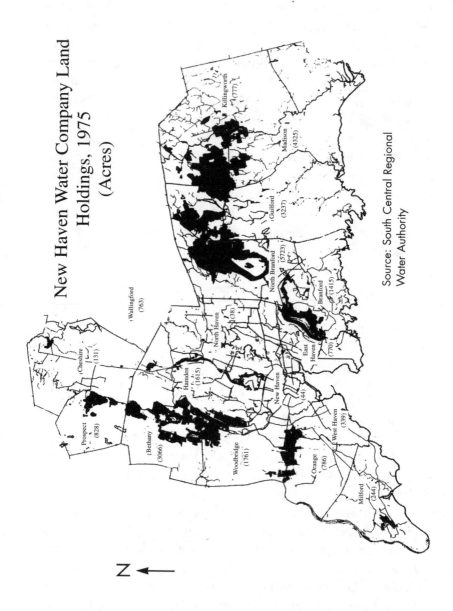

New Haven Water Company Land Holdings, 1975 (Acres)

Killingworth (777)

Madison (4325)

Guilford (3237)

North Branford (5723)

Branford (1415)

Wallingford (763)

North Haven (38)

East Haven (770)

Cheshire (131)

Hamden (1615)

New Haven (44)

Prospect (828)

Bethany (3066)

Woodbridge (1761)

Orange (786)

West Haven (339)

Milford (244)

N ←

Source: South Central Regional Water Authority

drinking water supplies. Over 60,000 of these acres were owned by private water companies, and lay within the densely populated Greenwich to Hartford urban corridor, where they constituted over 50% of the remaining open space. While the state, towns, and environmentalists saw the future use of water company land as protecting water quality and open space and providing opportunities for recreation, the private water companies saw it as a source of capital to meet filtration plant construction costs.

Whose business was it to resolve this land use controversy? Investor-owned water companies are very different from other private businesses. They enjoy the privilege of the power of eminent domain to help them acquire land to protect reservoir purity. They are authorized monopolies, regulated by the state public utilities authority, which allows them the opportunity to earn a reasonable rate of return to their stockholders. New Haven Water Company was chartered in 1849 by the General Assembly for the special purpose of providing pure drinking water.[6] Its charter empowered it to be a public service company in the water supply business. The charter did not authorize it to be in the real estate business, despite the fact that in 1971 the Water Company created a subsidiary holding company—the Eli Whitney Development Corporation. Clearly, it was the public's business to analyze the water company's claim that its land was surplus.

Future Use of Water Company Land: Liquid Asset or Public Trust?

New Haven Water Company officials felt that they had both the right and the need to dispose of lands they declared were surplus. They argued that many of their large land holdings were no longer needed to purify drinking water because of recent federal and state health regulations and the advent of new mechanical filtration methods. In order to finance the filtration plants, the Water Company argued that it needed to sell surplus land.

However, Connecticut's established public health policy was that it is safer to prevent pollutants from entering the drinking water supply in the first place than it is to try to clean up the water after it becomes contaminated. This policy recognized that undisturbed watershed soil performs the valuable function of natural water filtration.

Public health experts testified to the General Assembly's Environment Committee that conventional mechanical water filtration plants are not reliable in removing many pollutants, or are too costly, both to build and to operate, for general use.[7] Although conventional filtration and chlorine treatment kills bacteria and some viruses, it has no effect on other viruses, including hepatitis.

The federal EPA had recently estimated that one thousand new chemicals were introduced annually into the environment. One water quality expert commented, "There are more scientists making chemicals than there are scientists and regulators deciding if they are harmful".[8]

Richard S. Woodhull, Chief of Water Supplies Section of the State Department of Health, had warned New Haven Water Company President Woods in 1976 that:[9]

> Continued maintenance of water sources free as possible from pollution is necessary. Chemical pollutants such as salt, gasoline, oil, and trace toxic metals are not effectively dealt with by standard treatment methods, and therefore must be dealt with at the source on the watershed.

Concern over the proposed sale of surplus land triggered action by the 1975 General Assembly to declare a two-year moratorium on water company land sales and to create a Council on Water Company Lands to study the matter and recommend means of protecting the public interest in the proper use of this land. First proposed by attorney Russell L. Brenneman, former counsel to the Department of Environmental Protection, at a statewide conference in 1974, the moratorium legislation was sponsored by freshman State Representative Dorothy S. McCluskey (D-North Branford).

The moratorium was fiercely fought by private water companies. One of the opponents' most effective lobbyists, Thomas F. Dowd, Vice President of the investor-owned Bridgeport Hydraulic Company and a recent state senator, called it "unnecessary, unworkable and unconstitutional".[10] New Haven Water Company offered to voluntarily withhold land sales for two years.[11] However, the moratorium survived scrutiny by the legislature's attorneys, the state Department of Environmental Protection, and the Regional Planning Association of South Central Connecticut. Some years later, in response to a court challenge by the Bridgeport Hydraulic Company, it was upheld by the U.S. District Court and the U.S. Supreme Court. In his decision, Judge Zampano wrote:[12]

> It therefore seems reasonable that the State, having delegated to public service companies a valuable part of its governmental perogative to obtain land by eminent domain, should retain broad flexible authority to regulate and even delay any large abandonment of those companies' properties by open market sales. Economic, health and safety concerns justify the exercise of continuous and dominant police power by the State to safeguard against improvident decisions of public service companies.

The Council on Water Company Lands, chaired by Sarah M. Richards, a Guilford biologist, and made up of health, environmental, planning, and public utility control officials and citizens, immediately tackled the task of compiling an inventory of water company land, identifying which land, if any, might safely be sold, and addressed related legal and economic issues. Lacking any operating funds, the Council turned to the State Department of Health for office staffing and space, to Conservation Law Foundation of New England attorney Sarah M. Bates for legal assistance, and to other volunteers for professional consulting services.

Summarized in a February 1977 report to the General Assembly, the Council's research recommended setting up a land classification system for both privately and publicly owned water company land. The report stressed that conventional water filtration plants are *not* a substitute for the protection afforded by controlling the use of critical watershed land.[13]

The classification system divided water company land into three categories: 1) those that are necessary to protect pubilc health and must remain in water company ownership, 2) those that are not necessary because they are off the watershed and may be sold, and 3) the remaining bulk of the watershed land that requires use restrictions and can only be sold if granted a permit by the state Department of Health. The land classification was based upon the physiographic characteristics of the land, including steepness of slope and location of wetlands, characteristics which form the basis of the land's significance for protecting the public drinking water supply. Land located within the watershed but not owned by a water company was not subject to the land classification system. New Haven Water Company owned 24.5% of its public drinking water supply watershed overall, ranging from 73% of the Lake Saltonstall to $3^1/2\%$ of the Lake Whitney watersheds.

The proposed classification legislation was passed on the final day of the General Assembly's 1977 session—the same day that the regional water authority enabling legislation passed. It was signed into law (PA 77-606) shortly thereafter by Governor Ella T. Grasso, whose earlier endorsement of the proposal was instrumental in its passage. In a letter to the Environment Committee Co-chairmen in March she stated, "The State of Connecticut has a precious heritage in her water supply lands. I believe it would be shortsighted to allow the sale of critical protective water supply land holdings in order to obtain a one-time financial gain."[14] The private water utilities including New Haven Water Company, vigorously fought this legislation, although, interestingly, there was no opposition from publicly owned water utilities. In fact, the Hartford Metropolitan District Commission supported retention of watershed land.

What significance did the moratorium and the land classification have for public purchase of the private New Haven Water Company? By removing the immediate threat of water company land sales, the moratorium gave the affected towns 1) time to buy "surplus" Water Company land if they could afford to and 2) time to explore the possibility of regional ownership. By severely restricting watershed land sales, the classification law limited the Water Company's ability to use its land as a source of capital for financing construction. Consequently, public ownership, with its accompanying state and federal tax savings, became increasingly attractive. The issue of land disposal cried out for careful consideration.

Since consideration of both the proposed bill for classifying water utility lands and the bill for creating a South Central

Connecticut Regional Water Authority were being debated by the General Assembly at the same time, it was not surprising that some confusion resulted. Some legislators thought that the classifcation bill, because it greatly restricted land sales, eliminated the pressure for a regional water authority. However, it soon became apparent that the land sale threat was not the only factor favoring public ownership.

Financial Constraints: A Close Look At A Troubled Water Company

With a hostile regulatory climate, increased demands made by federal and state safe drinking water requirements and limited access to credit markets, New Haven Water Company faced an uncertain financial future. In 1976, the Water Company forecast that expenditures of $110,000,000 would need to be made to replace and expand existing facilities and to construct treatment plants.[15] This exceeded the total cost of the existing utility plant.

But how to raise the dollars? With a 60% - 40% debt equity ratio called for by its outstanding bond indentures, the Water Company was reaching the limit of its borrowing power. "From the [water] company's perspective, selling additional equity at below book value would have hurt the existing stockholders by 'watering down their stock' and Charles Woods, President of New Haven Water Company, really didn't want to do that if he could avoid it. The sale of the land, or ultimately the sale of the company, made much more sense from the stockholder's point of view than having the equity diluted", explained Vice President John Crawford.[16]

Without significant changes in the regulatory climate or economic conditions, investment analysts doubted the capacity of the Company to obtain the funds necessary to finance this capital construction program without incurring excessive financing costs, and subsequent rate increases, if funds could be obtained at all.[17]

So the Water Company resorted to selling land. The plan to put thousands of acres of land on the market, land acquired decades earlier at an average cost of $124 an acre—estimated in 1979 to be worth $3,158 an acre[18]—was made public. Even with the sale of land there was considerable debate about whether sufficient capital could be raised. The proposed sale of land became the catalyst for the moratorium on the sale of water company lands and led to the imposition of stringent land sales restrictions.

In an effort to make the firm's stock more appealing to investors some inventive, though unsuccessful, undertakings were attempted. In 1972, the Water Company proposed selling twenty acres in Hamden, at its original cost of $10,000, to a newly created real estate development subsidiary, the Eli Whitney Development Corporation, to construct an eighty-six unit condominium. The land had previously been turned down by the town when it was offered at its market value of $1,000,000. In 1973, an even more creative proposal was unveiled: a joint venture between New Haven Water Company and the New Haven Trap Rock Company to quarry 50,000,000 tons of a North Branford traprock ridge to create a 3,000,000,000 gallon new reservoir. Some of the rock would be quarried from the ridge land owned by the Water Company, and then sold to the mining firm.[19]

Added to the Water Company's financial woes, a long standing controversy over who should benefit from water company land sales was awaiting court action. Since 1972, Connecticut Department of Public Utilities Control regulations had required profits from the sale of water company land to benefit the ratepayer. Private water companies, protesting that the profits should go instead to the stockholders, challenged the state regulation. Stockholders' expectations of windfall profits from land sales were dashed in 1979 by the Connecticut Superior Court's decision upholding the utility commission's regulations.[20]

This decision dampened the water company's enthusiasm for land sales and enhanced the attractiveness to shareholders of a public buyout. Between 1976 and 1978 New Haven Water Company stock prices rose, as a result of market speculation in anticipation of the company's sale, from $40 to $69 per share with no substantial increase in the book value. Among those who stood to profit were Water Company President Woods, who had increased his holdings from 300 shares in 1975 to 1,978 shares in 1978,[21] and Joel Cohn, the Company's largest shareholder who controlled 22,127 shares.[22]

That shareholder profit from appreciated land values was the motivation for New Haven Water Company land sales was unmistakably declared by Woods at a 1974 Connecticut Forest and Park Association forum on this issue:[23]

> It is the basic policy of this company to dispose of its land, including that which is not necessary now or in the future for water supply purposes, including that over which appropriate control must be exercised for water supply purposes but for which ownership is not required, in a way that assures that the gains from such sales or other disposition will inure to the benefit of the shareholder. It remains the basic strategy of this company, within the constraint of this overriding policy, to have this disposal take place through an affiliated real estate company at book value, *or by any other means which will insure that these benefits do, in fact, go to the shareholder.*

Who would benefit from the windfall profits reaped from land sales under public ownership—Water Company shareholders or water consumers through lower rates or safer drinking water?

Public vs Private Ownership: What Advantages Are There to Public Ownership?

Nationally, 82% of all water utilities were owned by government agencies. Connecticut, with its fairly even balance between government and investor-owned water companies, was the unusual case according to the January 5, 1977 report of the Commission to Study the Feasibility of a South Central Connecticut Regional Water District.[24]

Under continued investor-ownership and assuming the Water Company was able to raise the necessary capital to finance its $110 million capital improvement program, the Commission concluded the Company would need to increase rates two to three times their present level. Rate increases totaling 48% had been granted to the Water Company in the past three years and in 1977 it sought an additional 25% increase. The Report estimated that the cost of water under a regional authority in 1985 would be about 25% less than under the Water Company and these savings could be passed on to consumers.[25]

The savings would result principally from:

> 1. A regional water authority would not pay the federal and state corporate income taxes, state sales tax, and state gross receipts tax that are paid by the New Haven Water Company—a projected savings in 1985 of $7,400,000.[26]
>
> 2. Additional capital improvements would be financed through the sale of tax-exempt revenue bonds and would be less expensive than the cost of raising capital by the investor-owned company.
>
> 3. The formula recommended by the Commission for payments in lieu of municipal property taxes would produce significant savings for water consumers compared to full property tax payments that would have to be made by the private company via taxable bonds or sale of stock.[27]

Keeping water rates down for consumers was a high New Haven priority. Higher water rates were inevitable—the amount of the increase was the variable. The absence of state and federal tax

"What about us?"

source: *New Haven Register*, 6 February 1977

payments was the foremost factor cited in arguing that public ownership leads to lower consumer rates. Since similar or greater reductions in consumers' water costs would result from either city or regional ownership, what other advantages were there to regional ownership?

The loss of water company taxes would have the most devastating impact on suburban towns. Although the City of New Haven indicated it would consider making payments in lieu of taxes equal to the amounts area towns were presently receiving, it had no legal obligation to do so. Under the proposed regional ownership the regional water authority would make payments in lieu of taxes on all property acquired, equivalent to the taxes that would be paid by a private owner. The payments would increase along with increases in tax rates and assessments, but would not be made upon any future improvements. Although this was "unacceptable" to many towns, it proved to be preferable to the alternative.

The possibility of the City, by exercising its 1902 option, owning 26,000 acres of land in sixteen suburban towns and controlling the water supply in twelve of the towns was the most frightening to many. Added to the loss of control over as much as a third of their community, was the vision of massive multi-family housing projects and the accompanying costs of providing municipal services to the new development.

Recreational opportunities were also a concern of urban residents. Opportunities within the City were limited by lack of undeveloped land and varied in the suburbs depending upon the landowner. "Lake Saltonstall In Its Heyday Was An Oasis For Tired City Dwellers" proclaimed a 1966 news headline mourning the closing of this East Haven resort popular since 1890 and accessible by railroad and trolley.[28] (see Appendix F) The private water utility was in the business of water supply, not public recreation and there was little incentive or justification for the expense of maintaining and policing fishing, hiking or hunting uses. Under regional ownership, every town would have a voice in the use and management of the property and opportunity to develop support for compatible recreational activities.

However, in the eyes of many local and state officials and area town citizens the overall advantage of regional ownership was that it was the only viable alternative to city control. The question facing us is "not public versus private ownership of New Haven Water Company, but rather which form of public ownership: city or regional", concluded Representative McCluskey, who represented North Branford on the Commission and who sponsored the state legislation creating the South Central Connecticut Regional Water Authority and led it through the legislative labyrinth.[29]

Regional cooperation needn't begin and end with water. Creating a regional water authority represented unprecedented cooperation between suburban and urban people of diverse and often divisive opinions. Perhaps it has opened the door for future cooperation in providing for other public services. By recognizing the interdependence of the city and its suburbs, it offered the hope of their working together in the future to resolve issues of regional concern.

With authorization for creating a regional water authority, the stage was set for negotiating public purchase. What was a fair purchase price? Who would reap the profits? With three players on the stage, the Water Company, the City, and the Regional Water Authority, there were no easy answers.

THE NEW HAVEN REGISTER, WEDNESDAY, APRIL 13, 1966

Lake Saltonstall railroad station and steamboat landing

Would land disposition prove to be either a panacea for the financial needs of the Water Company or a bonanza for the shareholders? The Water Company assumed land it designated as "surplus" could be sold at fair market value. By severely restricting the amount of land that could be sold, the land classification legislation drastically altered shareholders anticipated profits from land sales. By requiring that profits from land sales benefit ratepayers rather that shareholders, the public utilities authority removed much of the Water Company's incentive for selling the land. Thus, the undetermined and disputed value of the land as a source of capital became a major factor affecting agreement upon a fair purchase price.

The federal safe drinking water law, the Water Company's financial difficulties, the City of New Haven's purchase option, suburban mistrust of the city, federal and state tax policies, escalating water rates, and political maneuvering, all combined to make regional purchase of New Haven Water Company a reality.

PART TWO

Legislative History of South Central Connecticut Regional Water Authority

A Land Use Controversy Erupts

In 1974, one third of the town of North Branford—5,723 acres—was owned by New Haven Water Company. The Water Company had just announced that it planned to sell as much as 3,000 acres of what it considered "surplus" land in North Branford. Town officials and residents were shocked. They had always assumed that this land would remain undeveloped in order to protect the Lake Gaillard reservoir water quality. The largest reservoir in the Water Company's water supply system, this was the primary source of the City of New Haven's drinking water.

At the same time, the North Branford Democratic Town Committee, which had not had a winning candidate for state representative since 1884, was looking for someone to run for the state legislature. Previously, the Committee had asked Conservation Commission Chair and Planning Board member Dorothy S. McCluskey to become a candidate but she had declined. However, reflecting on the water company land sales threat, both to the town and to the state, this time she agreed to run. She made the water company land sales issue the focal point of her campaign.

Speaking at the 1974 annual conference of the Natural Resources Council of Connecticut, one of the state's most widely respected environmental attorneys, Russell L. Brenneman, proposed placing a moratorium on the sale of water company land while the "surplus" land issue was studied.[30] This proposal, along with the protection of safe drinking water, became the top priority of McCluskey's early work in the General Assembly.

A two-year moratorium on water company land sales was enacted by the legislature in 1975 after surviving the scrutiny of its constitutionality by numerous attorneys. The moratorium act (PA75-405) also created a Council on Water Company Land Sales charged with making an inventory of water company land and establishing criteria for determining which land might be surplus and not needed to protect water supplies.[31] This led to enactment in 1977 of a safe drinking water policy for Connecticut that established a landmark watershed land classification system. The classification system defined the relationship between the land and drinking water quality and severely restricted the sale of watershed lands.[32] (see Appendix D)

The concept of a regional water authority emerged early in McCluskey's legislative campaign through discussions with her Campaign Manager Attorney Pasquale (Pat) Young and Finance Manager Claire C. Bennitt. It seemed to them like a good idea but not a good campaign issue because of the complexity of the issues involved and the prevailing Connecticut perception that any kind of regional authority was a threat to home rule.

Suburban towns had jealously guarded their sovereignty from the threats, real or perceived, of land-poor urbanites seeking recreational and housing opportunities. Moreover, the doctrine that private enterprise operates more efficiently and effectively than public undertakings was firmly entrenched.

As it turned out, there was an even more ominous threat than land sales—the possibility that the City of New Haven would buy New Haven Water Company under a 1902 contract that allowed the City a purchase option every twenty-five years. When Mayor Frank Logue, in 1977, announced his intention to exercise that option, suddenly the concept of a regional water authority became much more palatable to the suburban communities.

It was still not easy to agree upon the mechanics, especially the voting rights of the representatives of the seventeen towns (Bethany, Branford, Cheshire, East Haven, Guilford, Hamden, Killingworth, Madison, Milford, New Haven, North Branford, North Haven, Orange, Prospect, Wallingford, West Haven, and Woodbridge), and the amount of payments in lieu of taxes to be made to the towns by the regional water authority.

Conceived as a compromise to resolve a land use conflict and to forestall City ownership, the Regional Water Authority's enabling legislation underwent a lengthy and stormy legislative journey and a most difficult birth.

Creation of a Regional Water Authority Feasibility Study Commission: The Threat of City Condemnation

Even authorizing a study of creating a regional water authority proved difficult. A bill to do this (HB7669) was introduced by Representatives McCluskey and Thomas Grasser (D-Wallingford) in January 1975.[33] At a public hearing held on it by the Regulated Activites and Energy Committee, favorable testimony was presented by North Branford Deputy Mayor Pat Young, Eugene Seder, Chair, Environmental Protection Association of South Central Connecticut, and attorney Peter A. Treffers, Clean Water Group.

But the legislature took no action on the proposal. However, enactment in 1975 of the two year moratorium on water company land sales, by removing the threat of immediate sales, gave the towns time to explore the potential advantages and disadvantages of a regional water authority. Several towns created water company land sales study committees.

In the 1976 session of the General Assembly, the regional water authority debate began dramatically. Without any warning to area towns, the City of New Haven introduced legislation giving the City the power to condemn the property of New Haven Water Company.[34]

The bill's stated purpose was to provide water to consumers at a lower rate and to enable use of the water company open space land for public purposes. However its impact on the seventeen area towns would have been enormous. Besides the loss of tax revenue and loss of control over use of the land, which would also occur if the City exercised its 1902 option with the Water Company, condemnation had additional significant disadvantages. Whereas the City option provided for negotiations between a willing buyer and a willing seller, under the redevelopment provisions of condemnation law, the participants would lose the right to negotiate. Instead, a court would decide the acquisition terms and price.

Calling it "a slap in the face" to New Haven area towns and to the Council on Water Company Lands, Representative McCluskey warned, ". . . it would preclude opportunity for a rational discussion of possible solutions to resolve the problems of all parties involved—the taxpayers, the ratepayers, the water company's need to finance construction and provide a return to stockholders, and the need to protect public health."[35]

Alerted to the condemnation bill, by a notice in the General Assembly's daily *Bulletin*, on the morning of March 8th when the Regulated Activities and Energy (RAE) Committee was to hold a public hearing on it, Representative McCluskey vehemently opposed it. Hoping to make it less of a disaster for area towns, she urged the committee to amend it (1) to protect the existing taxes to the towns, (2) to give first option to the affected towns to buy any water company land, and (3) to give the towns the right to approve any development of water supply property.

Warned by Representative McCluskey of the condemnation bill, the North Branford Town Council immediately passed a resolution opposing it. The Water Company was North Branford's largest industry and its largest taxpayer. Real estate and personal property assessment of the Company's holdings topped $11,000,000 on the 1975 Grand List—fourteen percent of the town's total tax base.

Two days later, the RAE Committee approved the bill, including Representative McCluskey's amendments, sending it to the House of Representatives for action. However, the favorable vote was by only five of the twenty-two members of the Committee, and in an unusual procedure, the Senate side of the Committee turned it down. Committee Senate Chair Paul Amenta (D-New Britain) opposed it questioning, since the City can negoiate to buy the Water Company in 1977 under its contract, "why come to the legislature and put the legislature in the position of blackmailing a private company?"[36]

At the North Branford Town Council's request, the RAE Committee agreed to hold the public hearing on the bill in North Branford on March 25th. For the Connecticut General Assembly to move its committee hearing from the state capitol to North Branford for the convenience of local citizens was unheard of in this suburban community if not unprecedented.

A crowd of one hundred filled the Intermediate School cafeteria. Officials from North Branford and other New Haven area towns voiced their strong disapproval of the condemnation proposal. The League of Women Voters testimony in opposition represented twelve suburban towns.

New Haven Corporation Counsel Thayer Baldwin, Jr. (also a former director of New Haven Water Company), testified in favor of enabling City condemnation, commenting that, if passed, the measure

Stirring Up The Waters

source: *New Haven Register*, 13 March 1977

would only "expand alternatives", referring to the City's contract with the Water Company.[37]

RAE Committee House Chair George J. Ritter (D-Hartford), who chaired the public hearing, also defended the condemnation legislation, chiding the area towns' officials for not being prepared with a proposal of their own. He urged the towns to take action instead of being content to let state legislators' votes be influenced by Water Company lobbyists. Furthermore, he warned, "We are recognizing what the dangers are of losing valuable land forever if some specific action, whatever that may be, is not taken posthaste."[38] Specifically, he urged Woodbridge First Selectman Russell Stoddard to discuss this issue with Mayor Logue prior to the Regional Council of Elected Officials (RCEO) meeting the next week.

Eugene Seder presented an alternative proposal for public ownership, prepared by the Environmental Protection Association of South Central Connecticut: purchase by a regional water authority.[39] Representative McCluskey endorsed this concept and proposed amending the condemnation bill to create a regional water authority providing for participation of all towns, protection of the existing taxes and a referendum on any future sales of water company lands.

North Branford Councilman Ronald McKosky (who had been McCluskey's opponent in the 1974 campaign for state representative) voiced the view of several in asserting, "I do not believe legislation should be introduced to take away property belonging to the private sector. . . It is un-American and against the free-enterprise system and I'm objecting to it on principle."[40]

The following week, at Russell Stoddard's request, the RCEO approved proposing legislation creating a commission to study the feasibility of regional ownership of the Water Company.

Mayor Logue informed the RCEO that, while he intended to exercise the city's purchase offer in February 1977, he would welcome regional control if it could be worked out.[41]

New Haven Water Company President Charles E. Woods advised the annual meeting of the company's stockholders that public ownership was possible but not probable, and that the Company was not taking a specific position on public ownership.[42]

Leaders in the House of Representatives agreed to introduce a study bill as an amendment that would replace the condemnation bill. Quickly passed by the House and the Senate without further controversy, Special Act 76-68, *An Act Concerning a Commission to Study the Feasibility of a South Central Connecticut Regional Water Authority*, was enacted.

Thus, the City of New Haven's condemnation proposal jolted the suburban towns out of their lethargy and led them to at least explore the possible benefits of regional ownership of the Water Company.

Feasibility Study Commission: Why Should the Private Water Company Become a Public Regional Authority?

When the Feasibility Study Commisssion (FSC) convened on May 26, 1976, Howard D. Brooks, a retired regional school superintendent from Orange, was named Chair.

The seventeen member commission, given eight months to report its findings to the General Assembly, consisted of one representative appointed by the mayor or first selectman from each town to which water was supplied or in which land was owned by the Water Company. It was directed to evaluate the feasibility of ownership and efficient operation of the Company by a regional authority, including the economic and social costs and benefits of public versus private ownership, with emphasis on the tax issues, present and future land use, and financing of future improvements.

Without any funds to accomplish this task, the FSC turned to the participating towns for contributions and eventually raised about $16,000 and the donation of meeting space from the towns, and clerical and administrative assistance from the Regional Planning Agency.

Additional support came from an unanticipated source. In March 1976, President Woods, who had been authorized by New Haven Water Company Board of Directors to do so, contracted with the consulting firm of Holt, Wexler and Associates to draft model legislation for a regional water authority, and subsequently to assist the FSC in conducting its study and drafting enabling legislation.[43] The FSC also hired the financial consulting firm Bailey, Moore and Glazer and attorneys Peter A. Treffers and Sandra Sosnoff to write the report.

An insightful overview and historical perspective of the FSC was made in 1992 by Howard Brooks:[44]

> We were united by purpose, mandate, and determination but sorely divided on certain issues. The two major regional concerns, ownership, and management of the water utility and ownership and preservation of its land holdings, of necessity were given overriding considerations. The structure and organization of the public utility was shaped in part by our concerns relative to its operating efficiency and its becoming over time, a politicized body. . . Even as we arrived close to agreement on structure and organization, we became hung up on representation, hence the weighted vote. We tried to balance a prevailing concern over land preservation and management with a necessary and appropriate consideration of the interests of the consumer and rate payer—therefore the dual mission stated in Section 1 of the enabling legislation.

Providing a pure and adequate water supply, while at the same time advancing the public interest in the conservation of open space and providing appropriate recreational facilities, received much attention. Since the Council on Water Company Lands water utility land classification and sales restrictions had not yet been adopted by the General Assembly and there was no assurance that they would be, the FSC included carefully crafted land use standards and disposition policies in its legislative recommendations.

Taxes or Payments In Lieu Of Taxes (PILOT) was the most difficult and divisive issue to resolve. Chair Howard Brooks pointed out that this issue "was never really resolved but was only finally settled . . . by obtaining a majority vote on a proposal unacceptable to some members."[45] Indeed, this proved to be a foreboding—PILOT became the major stumbling block to legislative approval of a regional water authority. Intense bargaining and further compromising by state legislators significantly altered the PILOT provisions and other recommendations of the FSC.

A special voting formula was designed by the FSC in order to provide fair representation for all towns without domination by any one town or group of towns, while at the same time recognizing the

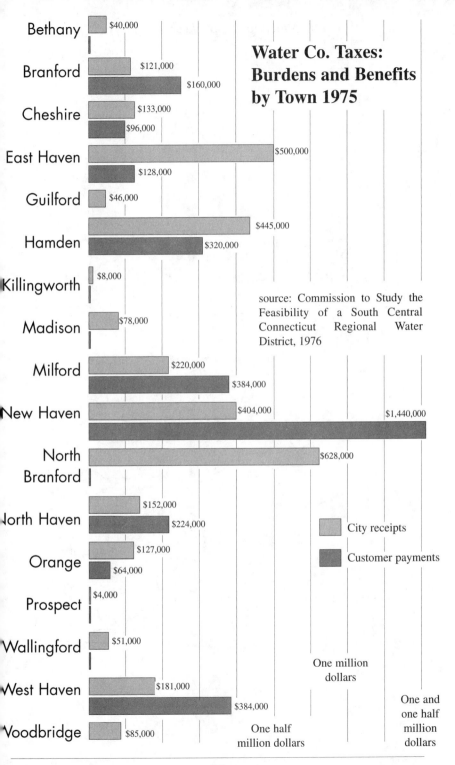

Water Co. Taxes: Burdens and Benefits by Town 1975

Bethany — City receipts: $40,000

Branford — City receipts: $121,000; Customer payments: $160,000

Cheshire — City receipts: $133,000; Customer payments: $96,000

East Haven — City receipts: $500,000; Customer payments: $128,000

Guilford — City receipts: $46,000

Hamden — City receipts: $445,000; Customer payments: $320,000

Killingworth — City receipts: $8,000

Madison — City receipts: $78,000

Milford — City receipts: $220,000; Customer payments: $384,000

New Haven — City receipts: $404,000; Customer payments: $1,440,000

North Branford — City receipts: $628,000

North Haven — City receipts: $152,000; Customer payments: $224,000

Orange — City receipts: $127,000; Customer payments: $64,000

Prospect — City receipts: $4,000

Wallingford — City receipts: $51,000

West Haven — City receipts: $181,000; Customer payments: $384,000

Woodbridge — City receipts: $85,000

source: Commission to Study the Feasibility of a South Central Connecticut Regional Water District, 1976

Legend: City receipts; Customer payments

One half million dollars · One million dollars · One and one half million dollars

25

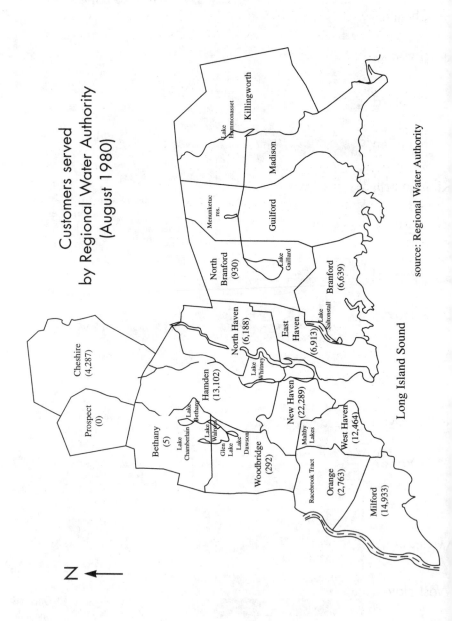

Customers served by Regional Water Authority (August 1980)

Killingworth

Lake Hammonasset

Madison

Menunketuc res.

Guilford

North Branford (930)

Lake Gaillard

Branford (6,639)

Cheshire (4,287)

Prospect (0)

North Haven (6,188)

Lake Saltonstall

East Haven (6,913)

Lake Whitney

Hamden (13,102)

Bethany (5)

Lake Chamberlain

Lake Bethany

Lake Watrous

Glen Lake

Lake Dawson

Woodbridge (292)

New Haven (22,289)

Maltby Lakes

West Haven (12,464)

Racebrook Tract

Orange (2,763)

Milford (14,933)

Long Island Sound

N

source: Regional Water Authority

relative importance of water supply and land conservation. The constitutional principle of one man one vote was not deemed appropriate because the Representative Policy Board, as compared to a regional school board, does not derive its revenue from tax monies, its members are not elected, and it does not exercise general governmental powers.

Regarding the future of current Water Company employees, the regional water authority would guarantee their jobs and assume their union contracts, but they would not continue to have the right to strike.

In analyzing the financial strength of the Water Company, it was found that the company was in critical need of capital. It projected the need to spend more than $110,000,000 over the next ten years and was reaching the limit of its borrowing power. Concerning water rate increases, the Commission forecast that in the future, under public operation, consumers would pay water rates approximately 25% below the level which they would pay to a private company.[46]

The conclusion of the Commission was that:[47]

> . . . regional ownership and operation of the Water Company is not only feasible, but vital to the health, prosperity, and environmental quality of the region, and in the Commission's view, far preferable to acquisition by any single municipality. . . .

> Therefore, the Commission recommends creation of the South Central Connecticut Regional Water District comprising the seventeen towns to which water is supplied or in which land is owned by the NHWC. The Water District would consist of the following:

> * the seventeen member Representative Policy Board appointed by the member towns with power to approve proposed actions relating to water rates, land use and disposition, and major capital improvement projects.

> * the five member Water Authority appointed by the Representative Policy Board charged with responsibility

for and broad powers to undertake the management and supervision of the water utility.

* a professional staff under the direction of a chief executive officer responsibile for the operation of the water utility.

Votes of members of the Representative Policy Board would be weighted in accordance with a formula designed to give each town's representative a vote proportionate to the number of customers residing in the town as a percentage of the total in the district, and to the acres of land held by the Water Authority in the town as a percent of the total in the district. Because the primary purpose of the Water Authority is to provide pure water at a reasonable price, the customer factor is given double weight in the formula. . . .

Until the Representative Policy Board adopts land use standards and disposition policies there would be a moratorium on land sales. Thereafter, the Water Authority could not dispose of land or change its use unless the Representative Policy Board found that the proposed action a) conformed to these standards and policies, b) was not likely to affect the environment adversely, particularly with respect to the purity and adequacy of both present and future water supply, and c) would be in the public interest, giving due consideration to the impact of the action on the consumer and on the municipality in which the land is located. . . .

Finally, the Commission recommends a formula for payments in lieu of taxes (PILOT) . . . that for a period of at least five years each municipality would, through PILOT retain its ability to generate tax revenues from its existing taxable property. The Water Authority would make PILOT payments on all property acquired equivalent to the taxes that would be paid by a private owner. The PILOT payments would increase along with increases in tax rates and assessments, with the limitation that the increase with respect to any property may not exceed five percent per year. However, no payments in lieu of taxes would be made upon any new improvements constructed by the Authority. At the end of five years, the PILOT payments would be frozen subject to the review and determination of a PILOT formula by the Representative Policy Board. Such determination would follow a comprehensive study of the effect of alternative PILOT formulas on member towns of the Water Authority.

When the FSCs struggles over PILOT, representation on the Regional Policy Board, and land sales restrictions had finally been peacefully resolved, the proposed regional water authority legislation was rushed to completion.

Awaiting hand delivery of the enabling legislation to Representative McCluskey at her Northford home, she and Administrative Aide Claire Bennitt were reminiscing about McCluskey's 1974 election campaign. They had been discussing Woods' voluminous and occasionally vitriolic personal letters disputing her remarks that Water Company stockholders stood to reap huge windfall profits from the land sales and charging her with "irresponsible" and "inflammatory statements".[48] Much to their astonishment the messenger who rang the doorbell was none other than a chagrined President Woods! That their conversation over a politely offered cup of coffee was constrained is an understatement.

On January 5, 1977, after nine months, over thirty meetings, and two public hearings in North Branford and in Hamden, the Feasibility Study Commission submitted its report to the General Assembly.

A few weeks later, the Council on Water Company Land Sales submitted its report and legislative recommendations to the General Assembly. As these proposals journeyed through the legislative labyrinth they were often interrelated and sometimes confused.

Enactment of South Central Connecticut Regional Water Authority Enabling Legislation: A Mazurka of Parlimentary Procedures

Representatives McCluskey (D-North Branford) and Gerald F. Stevens (R-Milford) and Senator Joseph I. Lieberman (D-New

Haven) introduced the Feasibility Study Commission's proposed legislation HB5995 *An Act Establishing a South Central Connecticut Regional Water Authority.*[49]

Before becoming law, the bill encountered a series of monumental obstacles, including becoming trapped in the wake of another bill's parlimentary problems. The legislative process is seldom an efficient, business-like procedure. (See "How This Bill Became A Law") Transforming a proposed bill into a new law requires conflicting personalities, principles, and policies to confront one another and to forge a compromise. Politics is aptly described as the art of the possible.

As a convenience for New Haven area officials and the public, the legislature's RAE Committee held a public hearing chaired by Representative McCluskey in North Branford on HB5995 on Valentine's day 1977.[50] Of the twenty-two speakers presenting testimony, most expressed acceptance of regional ownership as preferable to city ownership, but many sharply criticized the PILOT provisions or expressed strong preference for continued private ownership.

FSC Chair Howard Brooks emphasized there would be no loss in current taxes to municipalites and that the PILOT provisions were a compromise made by the FSC between no tax payments to towns under city ownership and full taxes under private ownership. Each town would receive payments in lieu of taxes equal to the taxes it was receiving from New Haven Water Company. These payments would increase, up to 5% per year, along with increases in tax assessments over the next five years. At that time the PILOT formula would be reviewed by the Representative Policy Board. However, no revenues would be received from future capital improvements made by the Regional Water Authority.

He also stressed that the investor-owned Water Company was unable to raise the necessary capital to meet their financial needs for the next decade.

North Branford Mayor Timothy Ryan called the PILOT provisions, which would pay no taxes on future improvements or construction made by the Authority, "totally unacceptable". A multi-million dollar filtration plant scheduled to be built in North Branford would become tax-exempt, resulting in a future tax loss to the town of $2,000,000 a year. Officials from Hamden and North Haven,

How This Bill Became a Law

House Bill 5995: An Act Establishing a South Central Connecticut Regional Water Authority

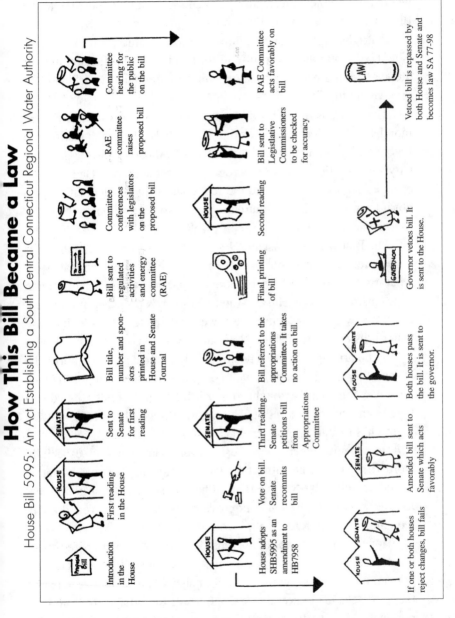

Adapted, 1995, from "How A Bill Becomes a Law." Prepared and published by the League of Women Voters of Connecticut Education Fund and the Joint Committee on Legislative Management of the Connecticut General Assembly

where improvements were also planned, added their opposition to the PILOT provisions, as did Bethany.

Outright support for a regional authority came from the City of New Haven and the towns of Guilford and Orange. Madison recommended adding provisions calling for a referendum in each town to give voters the final say.

The City's formal endorsement was a complete surprise. Eleven months earlier Corporation Counsel Thayer Baldwin had testified in favor of City condemnation of the Water Company. Now he gave the City's unqualified support to a regional water authority. Had the City changed its position? Or had the real goal of the condemnation proposal been to shock the suburban towns into getting their act together to come up with a plan of their own?

Mr. Baldwin emphasized New Haven's interest in reducing its water rate. He pointed out the cost of water in New Haven was twice what it was in Hartford where there is a publicly owned metropolitan water district. If New Haven Water Company's projected future construction over the next ten years were completed it could increase water bills by 200%, from $32 per quarter to $90 per quarter.

Summarizing the City's position on a regional water authority, he stated, "It's fair. It is a hard won compromise and we ought to bring ourselves together. We ought to buy it together. . .it is to the advantage of the customers and it is to the advantage of the region. . .the region has to start acting together."[51]

He acknowledged that West Haven, Hamden and especially North Branford, where the first large capital project was planned, would be hurt, but "North Branford has the same interest in preserving taxes on future capital improvements as New Haven does in reducing its water rate".[52]

House Minority Leader Stevens (R-Milford), in a prepared statement read by Representative Paul Abercrombie (R-North Haven), pointed out that the accuracy of the financial conclusions reached by the FSC depended upon its assumptions of the price to be paid by a regional authority for acquisition of the Water Company. He also questioned financing the acquisition by revenue bonds without necessiting a rate increase, noting that governments usually pay off revenue bonds from taxation if necessary. In addition he remarked that the recent report of the state Council on Water Company Land Sales includes detailed procedures for the sale of watershed land which, if implemented, "would very probably solve the environmental and land use concerns of the towns where the watershed lands exist".[53]

Sarah W. Richards, Chair, Council on Water Company Land Sales, pointed out the the land classification criteria recommended by the Council in its report and based upon protecting public health, would, if adopted by the state, apply to public as well as investor-owned water companies. She urged that this same classification system and policy for land disposition to be set by the state Department of Health, be used by the Representative Policy Board. In addition, she recommended that compensation be provided for Board members.

The RAE Committee scheduled a second public hearing at the State Capitol in Hartford on February 26th. This hearing was held jointly with the Environment Committee and included several bills proposed by the Council on Water Company Land Sales report. Some questions raised at the previous hearing were answered.

Mr. Brooks reported that the FSC estimated the Water Company purchase price at between $75-$125,000,000. The report was based upon a price of a $100,000,000. On this basis, the cost of water under a regional authority in 1985 would be about 25% less than under the Water Company.

The Water Company's public negotiating stand was revealed in the testimony of its Vice President John Crawford, "that if an institution can be designed that protects the consumer and the communities that we serve at the same time provides a return to our stockholders which is greater than they can anticipate under continued private ownership, then we would have an obligation to give serious consideration to such a proposal".[54]

Connecticut Water Company Vice President William C. Stewart opposed the bill, pointing out that as worded it was not limited to New Haven Water Company but would allow the Regional Water Authority (RWA) to condemn other existing water supplies within the district.

Subsequently, New Haven area state legislators met together informally at the Capitol several times to review and revise HB5995. Their discussion focused on the PILOT provisions which had become a stumbling block for the bill's passage. Representative McCluksey then drafted an amendment reflecting their consensus for submission to the RAE Committee. She had previously urged the RCEO to submit their recommended changes but they were unable to reach any agreement prior to the Committee's April 13th deadline for voting on committee bills.

On April 7th, the RAE Committee amended HB5995 and by a vote of 8-1 sent it to the Appropriations Committee. The amendment made the following changes: (1) deleted the five percent cap on annual increases in PILOT for the initial five years of the authority's operation, (2) called for PILOT on future construction during the same period, unless otherwise determined by the authority's Representative Policy Board, (3) exempted water companies from condemnation by the authority, and (4) provided per diem compensation for members. Three days later the RCEO finally reached agreement, but on a substantially different amendment that would (1) guarantee PILOT and (2) mandate a two-thirds vote of the 17 area towns to approve establishing a regional water authority.

Because it involved an appropriation of $250,000 in "seed" money for start up expenses, this bill had to go the Appropriations Committee for final committee action. However, a rare demonstration of unanimity by a Republican-Democratic coalition of thirteen New Haven area legislators failed to persuade the Appropiations Committee to support the request, or indeed even to take any action at all on the bill. Because of an inter-party budget block, the Committee had reached its May 1st deadline debating nothing but the budget bill.

Working to keep HB5995 alive, the bill's backers took advantage of a frequently used parlimentary procedure to petition it to the Senate floor, though with an unfavorable report from the Appropriations Committee. Unfortunately it arrived in the Senate shortly after the highly controversial "Bottle Bill" whose opponents had cited a little-known statute saying the Senate could not petition a bill sponsored by the House. Consequently, Senate President Lieutenant Governor Robert Killian (D-Hartford), referring to the "Bottle Bill" ruling, was forced to recommit the regional water authority enabling bill, in effect killing it.

Not willing to accept defeat, Representative McCluskey and other supporters searched for a suitable bill already on the House calendar awaiting action that could be amended with the RWA proposal. HB7958 *An Act Concerning Financial Assistance for Water Companies for Construction of Treatment Facilities*, which was one of the bills proposed by the Council on Water Company Land Sales, met this requirement. It provided for a Department of Planning and Energy Policy study of (1) the economic impact on water companies of the sale of water company owned lands and (2) construction requirements for treatment facilities and recommendations of possible forms of financial assistance for the construction of treatment facilities.

On June 6th, only two days before the General Assembly's mandatory adjournment date, the bill was debated and Representative McCluskey's thirty-four page amendment, which in fact became the bill, was introduced. During debate, Representative Richard E. Varis (R-Prospect), who later became Prospect's representative on the Representative Policy Board and Chair of its Land Use Committee for seven years, raised a point of order questioning the germaneness of the amendment, thereby placing the bill once more at the edge of defeat. Further debate was postponed until the following morning when House Speaker James J. Kennelly (D-Hartford) ruled that the point of order was not well taken. Citing Mason's Manual he said, "To be germane, the amendment is required only to relate to the same subject. It may entirely change the effect of the motion or measure and still be germane to the subject. An entirely new proposal may be substituted by amendment so long as it is germane to the main purpose of the original proposal."[55]

In introducing the bill, Representative McCluskey stressed that it would benefit all of the competing interests that are involved. It was supported by the RCEO, the City of New Haven, and New Haven Water Company. Acquisition would require the vote of the legislative bodies of 60% of the affected towns. The alternative of City ownership would be devastating to North Branford, where it was the town's largest industry and largest taxpayer and the tax loss of $700,000 a year would have resulted in a ten mill tax increase.

Debate was lengthy with many questions. Speaking in opposition, Representative Varis cited the revenue loss to the state of

$1,800,000 and the state obligation to guarantee any pre-acquisition bonds. Madison Representative Linda N. Emmons (R-Madison) pointed out that both the state and twelve of the seventeen area towns would lose tax revenue under City ownership, but regional ownership would prevent loss of tax revenue to the towns.

Oppposed by Appropriations Committee Chair John G. Groppo (D-Winsted), it was supported by Finance Committee Chair Gardner E. Wright, Jr. (D-Bristol) noting the fiscal impact existed because the City had the right to buy the water company. New Haven legislators emphasized the City would exercise its option if the regional water authority was not established. Representative William R. Dyson (D-New Haven) opposed it citing the lack of cooperation by suburban towns on housing and other regional needs that have put the City at a disadvantage. However, Representative Irving Stolberg (D-New Haven) argued it did not weaken the position of the City and described it as "a model for the kind of regional cooperation that is so desperately necessary to both cities and surrounding towns".[56] House Minority Leader Stevens, declaring his preference for private enter-prise, stated "I think I might summarize the feelings of many of us from the region by saying that it is a bad amendment and it should pass." Speaking more seriously he concluded, "I would support the amendment also as really the only alternative we have to an unfortu-nate situation".[57]

The amendment was adopted by a vote of 90-58 and the amend-ed bill by a vote of 120-5. Supsension of the rules enabled the mea-sure to be forwarded immediately to the Senate. There it encountered more parlimentary maneuvering. When New Haven Senator Lieberman proposed suspension of the rules to debate the bill, Senator Joseph P. Flynn (D-Ansonia) objected, forcing a tie vote that put the bill on the back burner with only a few hours left on the last day of the session. Senate President Pro Tem Joseph J. Fauliso (D-Hartford) rescued it by moving for reconsideration. Senator B. Patrick Madden (R-Woodbridge) explained it, and was supported by Appropiations Chair Robert D. Houley (D-Vernon) and opposed by Senator Flynn. Finally, the bill passed by a vote of 32-3 on June 8th—the afternoon of the last day of the 1977 session of the Connecticut General Assembly.

She Know Not What She Doeth

source: *New Haven Register*, 17 July 1977

Harry Wexler reported to the Feasibility Study Commission that the regional water authority bill had survived the legislative labyrinth though "shorn of any appropriation and slightly amended. That it passed at all was due to the persistence and parlimentary savvy of Dorothy McCluskey and Pat Madden."[58]

A Surprise Veto Brings Bitter Disappointment

Feeling that their work was done, supporters breathed a sigh of relief and returned to their normal daily responsibilities. They were badly mistaken as they were soon to discover.

Dismay and disbelief was the response of New Haven area town officials to Governor Ella Grasso's stunning veto of the Regional Water Authority enabling legislation (Special Act 77-98) on July 14th. The Governor's veto message voiced concern that the bill (1) empowered the Regional Water Authority to incorporate additional towns into the district without legislative approval, (2) would result in a tax loss to the state in excess of $1,000,000 annually, (3) required the state to guarantee up to $5,000,000 in bonds, and (4) did not provide for state participation in the development of the RWA.[59] (see Appendix E)

New Haven area town officials expressed bitter disappointment. Mayor Logue announced the City would go ahead with its purchase plans. Feasibility Study Committee Chair Howard Brooks scheduled a strategy meeting with the RCEO, but noted that towns were now left with no option for regional ownership. Despite its often repeated previous praise for private ownership, the *New Haven Register* finally, in a July seventeenth editorial, added its endorsement of regional ownership.[60] House Minority Leader Stevens said he would urge the City to extend its November 20, 1977 option deadline to allow the 1978 General Assembly to address the governor's concerns. Woodbridge Senator B. Patrick Madden wrote to the governor saying she had "foreclosed on the opportunity of 17 New Haven area towns to have a voice in the management of their water supply".[61] Representative McCluskey immediately began the uphill fight needed to gather enough votes to override the governor's veto.

Overriding the gubernatorial veto was considered unlikely. To do so required a two-thirds vote by both the House and Senate. Of the 712 bills passed during the 1977 legislative session, only 22 were vetoed. Historically, veto override attempts have been unsuccessful. Nevertheless, an all out effort was launched. Area legislators and town officials, including RCEO Chair Robert Johnson, wrote to Governor Grasso urging her to reconsider her position.

Why did the Governor veto the bill? Why didn't she notify the bill's sponsors that she had a problem with it? Should the sponsors have actively lobbied the Governor's office to ensure her support? Or was the Governor poorly advised? Was she unaware that the same state tax loss would result from the alternative of City ownership? Was she unaware that General Assembly action could not be postponed because the city option could not be extended? All of these questions haunted the bill's supporters as they struggled to revive the stricken regional water authority legislation.

Senator Lieberman and Representative McCluskey arranged a meeting with Governor Grasso at the State Capitol on July 20th to discuss the adverse impact of the veto with her and to urge her not to oppose an override effort. Attending the meeting were Senators

Lieberman and Madden and Representatives Rosalind Berman (R-New Haven), Benjamin N. DeZinno, Jr. (D-Meriden), David K. Dodes (R-Hamden), Dyson, Vito M. Mazza (D-West Haven), McCluskey and Geil H. Orcutt (D-New Haven), and FSC Chair Howard Brooks, RCEO Chair Robert Johnson and the Governor's Legal Counsel Jay Jackson.

The day before the meeting, Jackson released to the press his memo to Governor Grasso supporting the veto, urging an extension of the City option to enable the 1978 General Assembly session to provide "proper safeguards".[62] At the meeting, responses to the governor's concerns and objections were discussed. She agreed that the concept of a regional water authority was "a sound one" and became persuaded that her concerns could be addressed during the next session of the General Assembly. Participants came away from the meeting with a promise from Governor Grasso that she would not oppose an override effort.

At the General Assembly's "trailer" session on July 25th, the rules allowed only for adoption or rejection, not amendment, of legislation. In a joint memo to their colleagues in the General Assembly, Representative McCluskey, House Minority Leader Stevens and Senator Madden urged them to overrule the veto.[63] Noting that the governor agreed the concept of a regional water authority is a sound one, the memo responded to the governor's concerns: (1) any expansion of the present Water Company franchise area would require approval of the local legislative body, (2) since municipal water utilities are exempt from state taxes, city ownership would also result in a similar state tax loss magnified by the additional revenue loss to local area towns of more than $3,000,000 and (3) a state guarantee of funds borrowed by the RWA must be approved by the state Bond Commission, which can impose conditions on their approval.

In moving for reconsideration and repassage of the regional water authority enabling legislation, Representative McCluskey explained the veto would result in a devastating tax loss to the citizens of North Branford, and to city control of one third of the town's land area. None of the governor's concerns would be solved by city ownership and none would have an adverse impact on the state prior to convening the 1978 General Assembly, at which time amendments could be passed to meet her objections. Letting the veto stand would close the door to New Haven area towns on the opportunity to protect their tax bases through regional rather than City ownership.[64]

Noting that the bill was supported by the RCEO, New Haven Water Company and the City of New Haven, Representative McCluskey remarked, "This bill represents unprecedented cooperation and honest compromise among sharply conflicting and controversial interests —interests of the city and of the suburbs, of Democrats and of Republicans, and of private and of public institutions—all working together to resolve mutual needs".[65]

Other issues debated by House members included the guaranteed retention of watershed lands needed to protect drinking water quality, assurance of lower water costs to consumers, the potential profit to Water Company stockholders from public ownership, and the possiblity of extending the option deadline. Referring to a memo from FSC Chair Brooks, Representative Lavine (D-Durham) pointed out that the City's option could not be extended past the November 20th deadline without first obtaining the consent of the bondholders—a cumbersome procedure unlikely to result in consent.[66]

Reversing his previous opposition to the bill, New Haven Representative Dyson rose to support the veto override, remarking that this would mark the beginning of "work on agreeing on other areas".[67]

In urging his colleagues to override the veto, Senator Madden summarized its provisions, and also addressed the issue of extending the City option, pointing out that the "bond trustee for the bondholders has received advice that it would be imprudent to extend the deadline on the option beyond November 20; so there is no opportunity to pass an entire new bill next session".[68] Senate debate focused on the possible purchase price, the lack of PUCA control of rates, assurance of lower water costs for consumers, giving the public a voice in RWA land use and other decisions.

The House overrode the Governor's veto by a vote of 116-23, quickly followed by a Senate override vote of 27-5.

A Senate override required twenty-four yea votes. Anxiously awaiting the tally, then exhuberant over an apparent three vote margin of victory, Senator Madden blurted out thanks to his colleagues before the vote had been formally announced. Corrected by the Chair he exclaimed, "I think what I am saying is this is as hard as having a baby!"[69]

Having encountered and surmounted almost every obscure procedural hurdle in the legislative arsenal—from a split committee vote, budget block, petition ruling, recommittal to rebirth as a forty-two page amendment ruled to be germane and a gubernatorial veto—the legislation enabling creating a regional water authority became law as Special Act 77-98 *An Act Concerning Financial Assistance for Water Companies for Construction of Treatment Facilities and Creating a South Central Connecticut Regional Water Authority.*[70](see Appendix E)

PART THREE

Acquisition: What is a Fair Purchase Price?

Following the successful override of the Governor's veto, the South Central Connecticut Regional Water District faced the November 20, 1977 deadline when New Haven's option to purchase the Water Company was to expire. Allowed no infancy, the organization had to be up and running in a matter of weeks. Acting expeditiously, each of the seventeen towns appointed a representative to the Representative Policy Board (RPB) and on August 1, 1977, Chair of the RCEO Robert Johnson, Mayor of West Haven, convened the first meeting.

The following week, Howard Brooks of Orange was elected Chair and committees were formed. Highest priorities were assigned to establishing contact with the New Haven negotiating committee comprised of aldermen, city development officials, and representatives from the Mayor's office and to the appointment of the five member Regional Water Authority (RWA). The committee on the selection of the Regional Water Authority members, chaired by Donald S. McCluskey from North Branford, had compiled a list of candidates and on October 4, five members were appointed. Howard D. Brooks, a retired regional school superintendent and retired military officer, was to serve as initial chair. Staggered terms were given: John M. C. Betts, a retired United Illuminating executive; Joseph A. Cermola, a businessman and professional engineer; Claire C.

Bennitt who had served as Representative McCluskey's aide during the feasibility study and the adoption of the RWA's enabling legislation as well as the bill calling for a moratorium on the sale of water company lands; and G. Harold Welch, Jr. a well known community leader with banking experience. (The original five members served as a team for thirteen years until January 1, 1991.)

With the RWA in place, speed to acquire the Water Company accelerated. A one-room office in East Haven was rented to establish a legal residence for the water district and staff support was hired on a part-time basis. While maintaining contact with the City of New Haven negotiators, the RWA proceeded to put together an acquisition team in record time and began to secure funding. Bond counsel, selected by the RPB, was Day, Berry, and Howard and the RWA expanded this legal role to that of general counsel as well, with Isaac Russell and Martin Budd as the lead representatives of the law firm during most of the acquisition process. An engineering firm and financial advisors were needed to round out the team and selections were made after extensive interviews. EBASCO, a consulting engineering firm, was hired to review the R. W. Beck engineering study of New Haven Water Company conducted for New Haven.[71] Coopers and Lybrand were to be consulted on tax matters and to review accounting projections. Charles Woods and John Crawford of the Water Company were kept apprised of all activities.

The seriousness of the purpose—regional ownership of the Water Company—and the stress of meeting a deadline imposed by the City of New Haven's 1902 contract, did not prevent lighthearted incidents. The RWA turned to Wall Street to hire a financial advisor and the process had a decidedly humorous beginning.

The East Haven office was small by any standards, perhaps 400 square feet with a jog for the bathroom. It was furnished with second hand tables, desk and chairs resembling early attic. The building also housed a travel agency and insurance office on the same floor. Use of the RWA office was sporadic, the part-time secretary was there mornings and on meeting days there was evidence of use, but there was a great deal of speculation on the part of the neighboring insurance personnel as to the real nature of the business. The worst was confirmed for them when the RWA interviewed Wall Street. The appointments were set an hour apart, and the firms all hired limos—black of course—for transportation. As the vehicles arrived, spewing out men dressed in regulation three-piece dark suits carrying briefcases, for the questioning onlookers it was enough. SCCRWA had to stand for something covering its obviously shady connections.

Humor notwithstanding, the interview process of the financial gurus brought Morgan Guaranty on board as financial advisors with Perry Hall and Howard (Sandy) Curlett joining the team.

Funding for the initial phase of the operation of the RWA was obtained by a loan from the RPB for $7,500. The RPB had solicited funds from member towns, prior to accessing borrowings authorized by the RWA enabling legislation, agreeing to repay the "loans" at the time of acquisition. When the early funding was depleted, the RWA backed by the State Bond Commission, approved a borrowing of $160,000 to support the acquisition effort. Bids were solicited from Connecticut banks, and Colonial Bancorp, as agent for Second New Haven Bank, was low bidder with an interest rate of 3.27%. Eventually, borrowings to fund public acquisition reached the $1,465,000 level with interest rates up to 8.06%.[72]

Concentrating on reaching a fair price for the Water Company and how to approach negotiations, the acquisition team labored through November and early December to put together an "acquisition plan". Arrangements were made to meet jointly with the RPB prior to a scheduled December 29th negotiation session with Mr. Woods and Mr. Crawford, in order to bring member towns up-to-date on strategy.

On December 8, 1977 the Board of Aldermen in New Haven held a public hearing on municipal ownership of the Water Company.[73] Mayor Logue, in his testimony, cited three reasons why City ownership was now desirable—the instability of water rates with a 73% increase in four years, the availability of revenue bonds for financing, and the City no longer received free water. Deploring the projected rate increases to cover the costs associated with the Safe Drinking Water Act, Logue argued for public ownership to relieve the ratepayers, savings estimated to be 25%. Admitting his bias toward regional acquisition, Logue pointed out that "the time has come for action and the only remaining question is whether we will meet our responsibility. New

"We'd Better Beat Him To The Punch"

source: *New Haven Register*, November 1976

Haven supports regional acquisition of the Water Company. But, I believe that in order to ensure public acquisition, the City at this time should decide to offer to purchase the Water Company."[74]

On the same cold December evening that the joint RWA and RPB meeting took place, the New Haven Board of Aldermen met to consider the proposal to purchase the Water Company for $110,000,000. Over unfavorable odds, the city had gained an extension of its option to February 20, 1978, and now was moving to finalize plans for purchase, placing tremendous pressure on the RWA to complete an acceptable acquisition package prior to that date.[75]

In meetings with management of the Water Company during the fall, it had become apparent that one of the major concerns was finding a way to avoid tax liabilities. The possibility of the Internal Revenue Service recapturing $12,000,000 of accelerated depreciation and tax credit was very real, according to Woods, and at the $110,000,000 price discussed with New Haven, after the known liabilities and tax recapture had been paid, only $44,000,000 would be available for distribution to shareholders.[76]

On December 28, 1977, eighty-four days after its appointment, the RWA approved an acquisition plan. Later that day the RPB set a public hearing date on the plan for January 26, 1978. The plan called for a purchase of all of the outstanding stock for $76. per share and the merger of the Water Company into a subsidiary corporation to be formed by the RWA.[77] In January 1974, when the announcement concerning the sale of land was made, the stock was trading for $39 bid, $41 asked.[78] On January 28, 1978, the stock had risen to $61-$66.[79]

In determining the price of $76. per share, the financial records, earnings and dividends of the Water Company were scrutinized and compared with other water utilities. The result was to value the ongoing operating entity at $40 to $50 per share for the 528,000 shares outstanding. The balance of the offer per share was to compensate shareholders for the surplus land holdings for $19,000,000 and to assume $59,992,360 of known liabilities. The initial revenue bond issue was to include the purchase price, acquisition expenses of $2,500,000, a debt service reserve fund of $8,337,000, and $11,301,000 for one-year's capital expenditures.[80]

The method of purchase reflected the Water Company management's concern over tax liabilities. It was assumed, based on Coopers & Lybrand's advice, that a stock purchase would avoid or postpone federal taxes of $14,112,000 whereas, purchase of the assets would have triggered the recapture by the IRS; the tactic was to offer fewer dollars per share, while the shareholders would receive maximum advantage of these dollars.[81]

After vowing to themselves to accomplish regional acquisition with an impromptu pep rally on the front steps of 100 Crown Street and armed with twenty copies of "The Plan", the five-member RWA delivered the details to Woods and Crawford on the morning of December 29, 1977 at the Water Company headquarters in New Haven. To say the $76 per share price was met with disdain is an understatement. Woods and Crawford were hospitable but completely unimpressed. They did, however, agree to move the offer to the Board of Directors.

Meanwhile, back at New Haven City Hall, the $110,000,000 offer for the assets of the Water Company was moving through

Aldermanic channels. Two more hearings were scheduled before action was to be taken by February 20. Conversations with members of the Board of Aldermen and Cermola of the RWA indicated that cooperation in solving innercity problems by the water district member towns must be forthcoming before New Haven would give up its option.[82] The specter of a willing buyer willing seller relationship developing between New Haven and the Water Company was raised, heightening fears of a bidding war.

At the same time a proxy fight was about to begin with the City and the RWA as allies. The Directors had two offers on the table—one of $76 per share and one for $110,000,000—equating to $84.76. Their dilemma was to find the highest possible offer for the shareholders and their strategy was as follows. They rejected the $76.00 per share offer of the RWA and reconsidered extending the option "which could not be extended again beyond February" until July 20, 1978.[83] The momentum seemed to be shifting to New Haven. The RWA removed the February 1 deadline for the Water Company's acceptance of its offer and planned a schedule of action prior to the annual shareholders' meeting scheduled for April 17, 1978. Following approval of the acquisition by the RPB after a public hearing on January 26, town meetings were scheduled for ratification of the acquisition, which required 60% of the seventeen towns according to the enabling legislation. Final approval by the required eleven of the seventeen towns was accomplished with the town of Prospect's ratification. The New Haven Aldermanic Committee on Public Acquisition voted to reject the RWA plan by a vote of 6-1.[84]

In early March, the proxy materials of the Water Company were reviewed and the RWA established a subsidiary corporation, and most unusual for a public entity, developed its own proxy materials for distribution to the Water Company shareholders. It was decided to hire a solicitation firm in order to make an all-out effort. Two mailings and telephone contact were part of the strategy, as well as paid advertisements in the *New Haven Register*.[85]

Despite the RWA's herculean efforts to convince the shareholders of the validity and fairness of the $76 per share offer, it was overwhelmingly defeated.[86]

In order to prevent municipal ownership of the Water Company, the

RWA immediately turned its attention to New Haven in the event of the City's success in reaching an agreement with the board of directors. Negotiations regarding the turnover of the utility to the region were begun. Throughout the spring, the RWA met with the Aldermanic Committee to discuss procedures and price.

After years of conflict, in June of 1978, an agreement was reached for cooperation among the RWA, the RPB, and the City to guarantee regional ownership.

On June 21, the RPB agreed that one RWA member always would be a resident and elector of New Haven, appointed from a list of at least three names submitted by the City. Further, the RPB agreed that New Haven could nominate a member to each standing committee and any special committee overseeing capital improvements and that approval of the appointments by the RPB could not be unreasonably withheld. The City was granted the right to participate in the setting up and operation of the Office of Consumer Affairs. Moreover, the RPB agreed to introduce and support legislation in 1979 increasing New Haven's weighted vote to 22. In return for these concessions, a Special Committee composed of the Aldermanic Committee members, future city mayor John Daniels, RPB member Steve Darley, City Counsel Thayer Baldwin, and Albert Landino, described by Frank Logue as "married" to public service, was to recommend assigning its rights to the RWA after reaching an acquisition agreement with the Water Company. Should New Haven not reach such an agreement, the conditions were to remain in effect if the Board of Aldermen approved the RWA's acquisition plan.[87]

The threat of a bidding war behind, the region and the city moved jointly to redefine the role of the City in making plans for public acquisition of the Water Company. On June 26, the Board of Aldermen approved an offer to purchase the Company for $102,000,000 and to assign the purchase agreement to the RWA.[88] Mayor Logue transmitted the offer to the Water Company and for two months letters "clarifying" the offer were exchanged. In September, the Company made a counter offer which was rejected by the City. By late fall, an $89 per share offer was being considered by the City and on November 30 the RWA agreed to accept the assignment of the City's offer if the Water Company's Board of

Directors acted favorably.[89] On December 13, the Board of Directors met and rejected the offer by a vote of 8-3 and in January 1979 the Aldermen voted against extending the City's "last and final offer".[90]

The City and the RWA had both faced the problem of determining the value of the Water Company's extensive landholdings. In assigning dollars to the various components of the water business, both had used conservative figures for the land— some $18,000,000. The figure was based on the view that the land classification system resulting from the recently enacted legislation recommended by the Council on Water Company Lands precluded the realization of huge gains from massive land sales.

Representative McCluskey tweaked the Board of Directors with an op-ed article in the *New Haven Register*, calling for "No Handouts for Water Company".[91] (See Appendix F) Pointing out that placing an unrealistically high value on the land wouldn't blackmail the public entities to increase their offers, McCluskey blasted the Directors for corporate greed. The Directors responded with a full page ad—an open letter rebutting Representative McCluskey and largely blaming "irresponsible politicians" for their financial plight.[92] (See Appendix F)

There was no lack of inventiveness on the part of those pushing for public ownership at the utility. Determined to go forward, a group of dissidents calling themselves the Alternative Directors, headed by Betsy Henley-Cohn (Joel Cohn's daughter), Moishe Reiss, and Thayer Baldwin, was formed to supplant members of the Board of Directors. Thayer Baldwin acted as liaison to the RWA.[93]

Proxy materials were once again sent to shareholders. Prior to the shareholders vote scheduled for April 24, the RWA agreed that if the Alternate Slate of Directors were elected, the $84.76 per share offer ($89 per share before a 5% stock dividend) would be reinstated.[94] The group's effort was soundly defeated and on April 28, New Haven Water Company stock was trading for $51-$55.[95]

In May and June, public ownership appeared doomed. Then, the Water Company, reeling from a court-upheld PUCA decision that proceeds from land sales would inure to customers, not shareholders, became an aggressive willing seller. Enter Messrs. Philetus Holt and Harry Wexler again, sent as messengers to meet with the RWA with

Woods' terms of sale as of July 3, 1979. The RWA agreed to conclude an agreement of merger based on Woods' proposal.[96]

Seven points formed the basis for the final deal which took another fourteen months to conclude: 1) $83 per share, 2) retention of 624 acres of the Wintergreen lands for the shareholders, 3) proceeds from the Wallingford land condemnation then under court determination of price,[97] 4) refunds from an appeal against Prospect's tax assessments, 5) accrued dividends to closing, 6) merger to protect against tax recapture, and 7) Charles Woods to remain an employee.

As the RWA faced the complicated task of putting together a plan of merger, the Board of Directors of the Water Company decided Woods had gotten seriously out in front and interjected itself into negotiations.[98] A Director's Ad Hoc Committee, consisting of Gerald Fellows and Arthur Sachs, who had previously negotiated with the City to effect municipal acquisition of the utility, became frequent visitors to the East Haven office. Arguing New Haven Water Company was worth more than $83 per share, Fellows and Sachs insisted that the agreement between the RWA and Woods be amended. When they brought up the subject of how much the region could afford to pay, Joseph Cermola pointed to a bowl of apples on the conference table and said, "Just because I can pay $5 for an apple doesn't make it worth it. Don't forget that!"

By then, a familiar camel, land conservation, had its nose in the negotiation tent. The Wintergreen reservoir, no longer in use for drinking water supply, and its accompanying acreage were within the boundaries of the West Rock Ridge State Park. By law, the state had first refusal if the land became available for sale. By agreeing to exempt the Wintergreen system from regional ownership, the RWA in fact was agreeing that the 624 acres would be sold, presumably to the state, but in any case the proceeds to go to the shareholders. Claire Bennitt and Howard Brooks, in meetings with George Hancock, a consultant hired by the Water Company to value and expedite the sale of Wintergreen, and with DEP Commissioner Pac, became convinced there would be significant problems with the agreement leaving the proceeds of the sale of Wintergreen to the shareholders.

In meeting after meeting, Fellows and Sachs argued their case. Dollars per share and Wintergreen were the obvious sticking points.

Finally, on October 5, the RWA agreed to $85 per share for 554,000 shares of stock. Wintergreen was to be set aside in an entity to benefit the shareholders and if not sold to the state in seven years, purchased by the RWA for $3,000,000. The Wallingford, Prospect, and dividend provisions were the same. And Charles Woods would be hired as an RWA employee. It was also agreed that the Water Company would make its best efforts for the following three years to consummate the sale of Wintergreen to the state and that the RWA would have first refusal to purchase Wintergreen at the best offer from anyone but the state.[99]

For the next six months, lawyers, financial advisors, Water Company staff and counsel, engineers, and the RWA met to hammer out the details of the acquisition agreement. The RPB was kept up to speed on the progress being made and New Haven's Aquisition Committee, now made up of Thayer Baldwin's wife Judith Baldwin, Daniels, and Landino were informed of all developments.

Compared with the megamergers in the late 1980s, buying what one Morgan Guaranty wag called a "humpty dumpty water company"[100] was not a big deal. But it was complicated enough and it was all done in public. The preferred stock had to be purchased, leases had to be renegotiated, personnel and union contracts and policies had to be reviewed, paying agents hired, litigation explored, contractual agreements scrutinized. Davis, Polk and Wardwell and Hawkins, Delafield and Wood joined the acquisition team members to make the bumble bee fly. The five RWA members and staff crowded into the increasingly inadequate East Haven office to tangle with all the open issues: staffing, tax recapture, and financing being the major problems.

The RWA talked with key Water Company personnel during November and December, to reassure them of the intent of the public authority to run the business through professional managers. The question of personnel contracts, already negotiated with the Vice Presidents in the event the utility remained private, arose. None of the RWA members had any enthusiasm for contracts but their views were considered hostile and disruptive to negotiations. The RWA remained adamant. The situation was finally resolved by the Water Company's Board authorizing the purchase of annuities—a move which took much of the sting away for Marshall Chiaraluce, Richard McHugh and Donald Jackson, Water Company Vice Presidents.[101]

Wintergreen, too, continued to cause headaches. In order for its sale to go through, the state Department of Health had to approve its abandonment as a reservoir and the land had to undergo a change in use under the water company lands classification regulations. A public hearing was scheduled to address the matter.

As plans were made and opinions sought and gathered, it was apparent to all parties that another, simpler acquisition strategy had to be found. Dealing with individual problems such as Wintergreen, threatened to squelch the deal. On February 22, 1980, the RWA approved in principle a restructured agreement allowing for acquisition by merger of all of the assets of the utility for $93 per share— including Wintergreen. The stock was trading for $75 1/2-$79 1/2 on that date.[102] On March 7, the *Agreement and Plan of Merger of New Haven Water Company with the South Central Connecticut Regional Water Authority Inc.*, a wholly owned subsidiary corporation of SCCRWA, was approved and signed by the RWA and the Water Company.

The Agreement spelled out in detail the structure and conditions of public acquisition. A reverse merger was called for, with SCCRWA Inc. to be merged with and into New Haven Water Company;[103] $93 per share to be paid to the holders of common stock; the three classes of preferred stock to receive $108.64, $115 and $110; the effective date to be June 3, 1980 with provisions for extensions; the surviving corporation to be known as New Haven Water Company. Usual provisions for takeovers such as representations and warranties and resignations were included. The water utility's Board of Directors was to recommend favorable action by the shareholders with a two thirds affirmative vote of the outstanding shares required for ratification. RPB approval and 60% of the district's towns had to agree to make the agreement effective.[104]

At last it was time to come to terms with financing. Interest rates had been rising steadily for several months. The issuance of tax-free revenue bonds always had been contemplated for permanent financing, but now that the financial feasibility of public acquisition was being threatened by high interest rates, Alan Anders, financial advisor with Morgan Guaranty, recommended that Connecticut banks be approached to help with borrowings for bridge financing. The RWA met with Connecticut Bank & Trust Comany (CBT). CBT was unable to provide funds at less than 11 1/2%, the cut off for financial feasibility.

The RWA travelled to Wall Street to discuss bridge financing with members of the financial community selected by Morgan Guaranty. Firm after firm presented a grim picture involving high interest rates and the implications of the financial environment on acquisition and water rates. RWA members discussed the situation for several days with advisors and decided to request an extension of the acquisition agreement. On March 25, an amendment was adopted acceptable to the Board of Directors which extended the effective date to no later than December 1980.

Now with time to breathe, the RWA requested additional funds under the state guarantee and discussed the possibility of bond anticipation notes as well as short term borrowing for bridge financing. Morgan Guaranty and Day, Berry and Howard worked to position the RWA to be ready to close the deal as soon as interest rates moderated. It was determined that a negotiated sale for the first series bonds would best serve the RWA's interests. Kidder Peabody, First Boston, Goldman Sachs, and Salomon Brothers were selected as senior underwriters with First Boston, Kidder Peabody, and Salomon Brothers to be co-managers for the initial marketing of RWA bonds.[105]

RPB approval of the acquisition plan was sought in May, following weekly briefings of its Chair Nicholas Amodio. In June, the RPB agreed to the terms of acquisition. The Office of Consumer Affairs had to be established as called for in SA 77-98, prior to any rate hearing, and David Silverstone, former Consumer Counsel for the State, was selected as Consumer Affairs Officer.

The drafting of bond resolutions became the focal point for the acquisition team. Hawkins, Delafield and Wood, represented by Richard Sigal, Stuart Fuchs of Goldman Sachs, Martin Budd, Isaac Russell, Daniel Anthony, and Alan Anders worked diligently with the RWA to produce documents that would, in a large sense, govern the financial actions of the RWA for the life of the bond, as tests for the issuance of bonds and maintenance of operating funds would determine future water rates. Funds were to be established to protect the bond-holders and a trustee to have oversight on budgets was to be selected.[106]

By July 24, the necessary town approvals had been received. Only Woodbridge and Prospect disapproved the acquisition and only Killingworth took no action. By then it had been decided to issue Special Obligation Bonds to defease the Water Company mortgage bonds. Discussions were ongoing with Water Company management concerning personnel, operational, and accounting policies. The physical plant was being gone over by Jeffrey Clunie of R. W. Beck. The rating agencies were given tours of Water Company facilities and all the information needed to provide ratings for RWA bonds.

The day the rating agencies were to tour the Water Company facilities could only be described as abysmal by lay people; Water Company officials said they were "taking a delivery". It poured from early morning on. Because the agencies did nothing together, RWA members and management split up, some were with Standard & Poor's and some with Moody's. When it was time to go to lunch, Joseph Cermola and Claire Bennitt got into Charles Woods' car with Mr. Ingrassia from Standard & Poor's. Woods took off for the Quinnipiack Club and when he got to the Brewery Street Post Office, the street was flooded. That didn't stop Woods, who plowed into the water at a great clip—only to stall—with water and sewage from the bypassed nearby treatment plant nearly up to the doors. Since none of the passengers volunteered to wade in the disgusting water, Woods opened the window and yelled at a bystander at the Post Office, "Call the Water Company and have them send a truck to get us out!" The response was perfect. "Why? It's not their fault!"

Subsequently, an A rating was received from both Moody's and Standard & Poor's for revenue bonds and an AAA rating for the Special Obligation Bonds.

Necessary final approvals were sought. The Board of the Water Company recommended approval of the $93 per share offer and at the final annual meeting of the investor owned utility, shareholders overwhelmingly voted to move the Water Company into the public sector.[107] The RPB selected Coopers and Lybrand as auditors, approved the bond resolutions and issuance of bonds and a rate increase of 14.5% to support the acquisition and the 1980-81 capital improvement program. Charles Woods was approved as CEO.[108]

By the end of July, market conditions had improved sufficiently for Goldman Sachs to recommend a bond issue to finance acquisition and an official statement was prepared. The revenue bonds were priced at 9.37% TIC over twenty-three years six months and a NIC of 9.6%. The bond purchase contract for $161,830,000 revenue bonds was signed and public acquisition was guaranteed.

On August 26, 1980, two years after the override of the governor's veto and after answering the question "Does anyone know of any reason not to close?" with a resounding "NO", the deal was consummated in Hartford at the offices of Day, Berry and Howard.

But at what cost? The $93 a share translated into an initial bond issue of $161,830,000. The components of the issue included $51,559,000 for common stock, $14,996,000 for preferred stock, $60,618,000 for mortgage bonds, $4,620,000 for prepayment of existing taxes, $3,600,000 for tax liabilities, $22,230,000 for establishment of funds required by the bond resolution, $1,465,000 for repayment of preacquisition loans, $12,840,000 for one year's capital improvement program and $3,958,000 for the cost of issuance. The 14.5% rate increase necessary to support the issue was considerably less than the 28% rate increase approved by management of the utility in May and forwarded to the Department of Public Utility Control (DPUC).[109]

PART FOUR

Transition: The Changing of the Guard

Opponents of regionalization of the New Haven Water Company had argued vehemently that public ownership would doom the utility to inefficiency and eventually to a bureaucratic morass. Proponents had argued with equal force that, with a structure designed to prevent politicization with the RWA as a buffer between the RPB and management, with tax exempt bonding available and the stated intent that the RWA would operate the Water Company with professional management, success was inevitable.

Would the doom and gloom experts prove to be right? How would the transition be made? Could the bumblebee fly?

Chief Executive Officer Charles Woods was fond of saying "water runs down hill". In the context of moving from an investor to a publicly owned utility, his comment could be construed to mean, "you guys can't mess it up too badly". A non-issue of some importance was put to rest during heated discussions by RWA members and its acquisition team concerning the perception of public management. New Haven Water Company was an old and distinguished name. SCCR-WA, an impossible acronym, was untried and unknown. For purposes of continuity, and to cause the least disruption possible, the RWA elected to do business as New Haven Water Company and continued to do so until late in 1982. Agreeing at least temporarily with Woods, many of the nay sayers took a modicum of comfort in this move.

As far as operations were concerned, water did indeed flow downhill. Pipe was laid, meters read, bills sent out, water treated, payrolls met, and phones answered—all as before.

However, retaining top management, developing the office of consumer affairs, public bidding, filing liens, finances and rate making, development of the long awaited Land Use Plan, and sale of the Wintergreen property were challenging and complex transitional issues requiring attention and diplomacy.

During the acquisition phase, the RWA had addressed the issue of retaining senior management. Meetings were held individually with key personnel including Woods, John Crawford, Richard McHugh, Donald Jackson, and Marshall Chiaraluce to reassure them of the RWA's intent to use professional staff to run the utility. Woods, as noted in the Acquisition Agreement, was to remain as CEO until 1982. John Crawford decided to leave and subsequently became a partner in the consulting firm Holt, Wexler and Associates. (Thirteen years later, on July 18, 1994, Crawford became the Regional Water Authority's third CEO.) McHugh, Jackson, and Chiaraluce remained with the RWA as Directors of Engineering, Operations, and Administration. For a period of time Gerald McCann, a former DPUC Commissioner, was Director of Finance. Woods' managerial style created friction McCann couldn't tolerate and he left the RWA starting what the local newspapers called "the Executive Drain".[110]

Relations between Woods and the RWA were strained from the beginning. Woods had little confidence in the RWA and alternately challenged its authority and ignored direct instructions.[111] As early as October of 1980, the RWA had to tell Woods that it was to be informed of any operational changes resulting from public ownership prior to their being initiated. Complaints regarding water main relocation costs unilaterally levied had reached Joseph Cermola, and Woods justified his unauthorized actions to the RWA by claiming his "right" to do so because of the change in ownership of the utility.[112]

In May of 1981, the matters reached a head: Woods granted a derogatory interview to the *New Haven Register* which appeared as the featured article in the Sunday Business Section. Erroneously claiming the RWA made all decisions unanimously and with difficulty, Woods said he had "to deal with decision demanding situations which remain in limbo for months as the Authority debates the issue without total agreement. I can live with a yes, I can live with a no, but I need a decision."[113] He had a decision instantly. The RWA immediately started a nationwide search for a new CEO, hiring John Crawford to help with a job description and to screen candidates. Woods resigned in June and Richard McHugh was appointed acting CEO and then in August as the second CEO one year into public ownership.

With the RWA's enabling legislation cutting the apron strings of DPUC regulation, the RPB assumed that role. Responsible for the establishment of an independent Office of Consumer Affairs, the RPB had appointed David Silverstone as the first to hold office, an attorney knowledgeable about both rates and representing the interests of consumers. The Consumer Affairs Committee of the RPB, one of the standing committees called for in the enabling legislation, adopted procedures for handling high bill complaints and termination of service and began functioning as a review board consumers could turn to after exhausting remedies available through the RWA and the Office of Consumer Affairs.

A significant provision of the enabling legislation was one requiring public bidding of all purchases estimated to be over $5,000. There was a further provision for waiving or exempting bidding but the RWA chose to walk a fine line. Procedures had to be established to implement the process and considerable time and effort went into making the money saving device meaningful and acceptable. Assuredly, vendors were alarmed at the possibility of losing certain sales, and personnel and the RWA scrutinized both the bidding and the exempting very closely. The facts that the low bid was not always the wisest choice and that negotiated purchases could be made, heightened the tension. As with most unknowns, the perception was worse than the reality and within a year the bidding tradition had good roots.

Another key provision of SA77-98 authorized the RWA to file a lien on property if a water bill remained unpaid. The RWA was one of the first utilities to have this option. Designed to ensure payment for product provided, the right to lien was implemented by notifying local attorneys that prior to a real estate closing the lien must be discharged. Over time it became accepted practice to include a search for liens as part of the master check list.

The finances of the public utility required adjustments. An annual operating budget and a one year capital improvement budget were to be prepared by the RWA as well as a five year projection of capital expenditures including improvements, additions, and renovations. The annual operating and maintenance and capital budgets were to be reviewed monthly. The rate making procedure called for the RWA to adopt rates and charges to cover operating expenses, debt service, Payments In Lieu Of Taxes (PILOT) and any reserve requirements and to maintain debt service coverage equal to 110% after PILOT and 125% before PILOT. Under the legislation, the RPB "shall approve such rates and charges proposes...unless it finds that such rates and charges will provide funds insufficient for, or in excess of the amounts required to meet all expenses of the Authority and the requirements of the Bond Resolution".[114] In 1980, the rate increase was 14.5% and in 1981, 10.8%. Fund accounting was to become the order of the day for the finance department.

Perhaps the most far reaching and significant regional effect of public ownership of the RWA was the use of the 25,000+ acres of land acquired. Guided by the Land Use Plan called for in the enabling legislation, in 1983 the RWA began opening lands previously closed to the public for recreation. This action fulfilled the dreams of many of the original supporters of both city ownership and regionalization of New Haven Water Company.

Putting together the Land Use Plan was a significant challenge — a joint venture of staff, the five member RWA, and the RPB. Starting in the fall of 1980 with familiarization of the holdings, the RWA toured all the properties by van and flew over the vast tracts of open space with Otto Schaefer acting as guide. From his intimate knowledge of the land and its history and his forestry background, came a vision for the future. Frances Ludwig, a staff environmental analyst, added writing ability and organization to the effort.

Required to develop standards for land use and policies regarding disposition, the RWA over a period of two years, an interminable number of meetings, several drafts, and dozens of maps, put together a document ready for public scrutiny.

The first section outlined criteria for land use. "The basic standard that guides the Land Use Plan is the protection of public drinking water supplies."[115] Goals were identified:

• To ensure an adequate supply of pure drinking water at reasonable cost;

• To protect outstanding natural and historical features;

• To reserve land for the production of timber, cultivation of agricultural crops, and conservation of wildlife;

• To manage nonrenewable natural resources judiciously;

• To match regional and local recreational and open space needs with land capabilities;

• To foster use of the land for education and research, especially for activities that will enhance awareness and understanding of water resources and improve their management and stewardship;

• To promote the development at appropriate locations of special institutions and facilities that will serve regional and local needs;

• To structure recreational activities so that they are self-supporting;

• To structure other land use activities so that they produce revenues in excess of costs;

• To provide sufficient flexibility to accommodate unanticipated future needs by exercising caution in committing land to irreversible uses.[116]

Five separate categories of land use were outlined:

• water supply facilities and source protection;

• preservation;

• recreation and education;

• natural resource development and conservation;

• and other land development.

Disposition and acquisition policies were established. Each of the discrete systems had individual plans: North Branford, Saltonstall, Mill River, West River, Racebrook, Maltby, North Cheshire, Pisgah Brook, Wintergreen, Prospect, Beaverbrook, and the miscellaneous parcels.

Ambitious in concept and detailed in presentation, the Land Use Plan called for opening lands cautiously for hiking, fishing, horseback riding, cross country skiing, and jogging. A permit system was designed to pay for upkeep and to control access.

The RWA held ten public informational meetings attended by more than nine hundred people. Following revisions to reflect public comments, on August 23, 1983 the Land Use Plan was formally adopted and sent to the RPB for approval. After two public hearings were held, the go ahead to "govern use and to determine disposition of all Authority holdings" was given by RPB approval on March 3, 1984.[117]

The final key in the transitional phase was another land issue. Some $3,000,000 of rate payers money was tied up in real estate as a result of the final acquisition agreement. The Wintergreen problem was not going to disappear magically. The RWA determined to continue prodding Department of Environmental Protection (DEP) in order to move the parcel into the state-held West Rock Ridge Park holdings.

In December of 1980, Bennitt and Brooks met with DEP Commissioner Stanley Pac to ascertain the state's interest and its ability to fund the purchase. Pac made it clear that the state desired ownership but that no money was available. The next step was to talk to Mayor Harris of Hamden, where the land was located, to line up support for the sale to the state. The RWA was convinced, after a meeting with Hamden's Mayor Harris, that the town would favorably view state ownership and would support efforts to make it possible. Then, a legislator had to be found willing to introduce a bill in Hartford to provide the necessary funding. He turned out to be Senator Eugene Skowronski. Because of the dollars involved and the relative ease of dividing the 624 acres into discrete parcels, the RWA informed DEP and the Environment Committee of the General Assembly that a phase by phase acquisition plan for Wintergreen would be acceptable if a formally executed agreement on price and timetable could be reached. A Memorandum of Agreement was signed on August 3, 1983 which called for the state to purchase all the Wintergreen lands over a period not to exceed eight years. The issue of which act prevailed—the RWA's or West Rock Ridge State Park's—for terms of acquisition was resolved by a legal opinion from Day, Berry & Howard: in the sale of any RWA land, Section 18 of SA77-98 was to be followed.[118]

State ownership was not to come easily, even after the signing of a Memorandum of Agreement and approval by the RPB. The agreement called for independent real estate appraisals by the RWA and DEP and they came in widely apart. How to reconcile the two took more than a year. Negotiations ranged from RWA headquarters in New Haven to the Governor's office in Hartford. The Office of Policy and Management (OPM) refused to allow the total amount of bonds for the first two parcels to go on the State Bond Commission agenda, stating the policy of never paying more than the state appraisal price for real estate. The RWA mounted a campaign to build public pressure for resolution of the impasse. To move along the process, in December 1983, the RWA offered to lower the price of all the remaining Wintergreen parcels to $2,507,000.[119] After a holdup by Jay Jackson in the Governor's office, the same Jay Jackson who in 1977 had advised Governor Grasso to veto the enabling legislation, the first two parcels finally were acquired by the state in March of 1984. On January 20 in 1987, seven years after public ownership, the State took title to the last of the Wintergreen land. The total price paid was $3,635,773.[120]

The Wintergreen saga had a happy ending. All 624 acres were to remain as permanently dedicated open space within the Park. The secondary mission of the RWA was upheld and the ratepayers and conservationists came out winners.

The bumblebee had taken off.

PART FIVE

The Sleepy Old Water Company as a Vibrant Public Agency

In 1996, with state of the art filter plants on line, stable rates, and an efficient productive workforce, the South Central Connecticut Regional Water Authority is in the enviable position of being able to meet head on regional challenges such as land use, hazardous waste disposal, recreation, and environmental education. At the same time that the buzzword "privatization" is heard everywhere, the RWA stands as an outstanding example of a responsive, responsible, regional government entity: since 1980, the organization has been living up to the expectations of its early advocates, even though many of them were unaware of its full potential.

When the debate was raging in the 1970s over regional versus municipal ownership of New Haven Water Company, little was said about a very real issue—the efficient delivery of services on a regional basis. The emphasis then was all on the prevention of one city owning the utility, lock, stock, and twenty-five thousand acres of land.

The case for regionalization of many services is not difficult to make. Watersheds do not recognize political boundaries. Aquifers exist apart from the political spectrum. Water mains do not stop at town lines. The protection of drinking water sources takes place on a system wide basis. The collection of household hazardous wastes town by town is not cost effective. A regional recreation system crossing town boundaries creates opportunities that are lost if planned with a municipal approach. Individual towns provide schools, but environmental education is concerned with issues.

Twenty years have passed since the City of New Haven began deliberations on public ownership of New Haven Water Company and the federal Safe Drinking Water Act regulated the filtration of surface water supplies. However, the two decades have not erased the memory of threatened land sales to pay for filtration plants, and capital expenditures remain near the million dollar a month level. Retention of public water supply watersheds for water quality protection and open space, the need to control development over drinking water sources, the demand for recreational facilities for growing populations, and the call for education on water resources and other environmental subjects are very much alive.

Today, the Regional Water Authority is not alone in its quest to control development on watersheds. Right now, New York City is in a fight to preserve its water quality by a "filtration avoidance program".[121] An editorial in *The New York Times* cries "Save the Watershed."[122] With vast reservoir systems beyond its boundaries, the city must convince its upstate neighbors that it is in the public interest to limit development that could compromise water quality, even if it means loss of tax revenue. With billions of dollars of projected capital costs and millions in incremental operating expenses, New York has incentives for solving potential water quality problems by requiring appropriate land uses and acquiring additional watershed land.

In the 1970s, Connecticut addressed the issue of watershed controls through a land classification system, but stopped short of state regulations to control lands not owned by water utilities. At the time the enabling legislation for the Regional Water Authority was drafted, public policy had not been developed for aquifer protection. Consequently, there were not the same stringent controls on land uses over underground water supplies as on watersheds. While adhering to legislative intent, the RWA moved early to establish an active source protection program with site plan reviews, watershed inspections, water quality monitoring, and education.[123]

Although most of the RWA drinking water is supplied by reservoirs, two of the district towns, Hamden and Cheshire, receive water from wellfields. In Cheshire, 80% of the residents are served by the RWA and between 60 and 70% of their water comes from the North Cheshire wellfield. At the northern boundary of the district, four wells are capable of producing 5,500,000 gallons a day. But of the 600 acres in the cone of influence, only 115 are actually owned by the RWA. The discrepancy in acreage sowed the seeds of conflict between town and water supplier similar to New York's.

In the 1970s and the 1980s, contamination was detected in the North Cheshire wellfield and "cleaning up contaminated surface water is child's play in comparison to cleaning up polluted groundwater".[124] An industrial solvent (TCE) and an agricultural pesticide (1,2-DCP) were found in drinking water samples. Hydrogeologic investigations revealed the TCEs coming from the north and the 1,2-DCP coming from the south where a strawberry farmer had used Vorlex. By 1986, at a cost of $1,500,000, an aeration tower was built to remove the contaminants from the water.

Additional measures for aquifer protection were in order as thousands of other chemicals in common usage might not be removed by expensive remedial action the RWA had taken. In 1986, the State of Connecticut recommended that municipalities revise their plans of development, substituting low risk land uses for existing high risk industrial areas over public drinking water supply aquifers. In addition, the towns were exhorted to strengthen existing aquifer protection regulations.

The RWA, already involved in the legislative process of the regulation of development, stepped up its efforts in aquifer mapping and watershed inspections. Determining that it was not financially feasible to purchase all the land in the cone of influence, in 1987 the RWA requested Cheshire to revise and strengthen its zoning regulations, arguing that the revision could enhance property values. Cheshire was dissatisfied with the proposal and asked for one allowing more varied development. In 1988, a new plan was submitted to the town allowing for mixed-use zoning and providing revisions to the existing aquifer protection regulations. In 1989, after property owners had opposed the RWA's proposal, fearing decreased land values, less restrictive regulations were put forward by the landowners. The town of Cheshire suggested that it was time for a compromise.

Unable to reach agreement, the matter went unresolved and Cheshire recommended postponing doing anything until model regulations, called for by the state legislature, were developed by the Department of Environmental Protection. Because of constant delays by DEP in drafting a model, for three years the matter was in limbo with frustration growing for land owners who could not sell or develop their land, for the town whose zoning regulations were unable to protect the water supply or satisfy residents, and for the RWA who had the responsibility and the expense of delivering safe drinking water. In the fall of 1992, officials from Cheshire met with the five member Regional Water Authority to discuss the problem. The RWA made it clear that large land purchases by the Regional Water Authority or ownership of development rights to much of the cone of influence were not the solution. With the RWA claiming that Cheshire needed to turn to the state for faster action in implementing legislation designed to protect its aquifers, the meeting ended in a standoff.

Despairing over the state's ability to act, in 1993 a new set of local aquifer protection rules were drawn up by the town. The RWA's comment at a public hearing was that the new regulations would "contribute to a level of protection not currently provided by Cheshire's existing regulations". The new regulations were adopted after public comment and are presently in effect. The town and the utility had managed, over a period of years, to hammer out a compromise to the advantage of the consumer, the residents and taxpayers, and the land owners.[125]

Another one of the persistent problems the RWA presently faces is unauthorized dumping on its largely rural and remote properties. The potential for substances hazardous to the water supply to find their way to roadsides and watershed hidden from public view is always threatening. With this in mind, a regional program for disposing of household hazardous waste was developed in 1989 in cooperation with the Regional Council of Governments (RCOG). Connecticut had a reimbursement formula for towns that conducted household hazardous waste collection days and many of the communities within the Regional Water District took advantage of the opportunity to host collection days. It was an expensive venture for the state and to the RWA and RCOG seemed an inefficient way to deliver a service. It made much more sense for towns in the region to band together and support a center that would be open for consecutive Saturdays to receive residents' household waste, instead of each town setting aside one day a year.

The RWA had land which could be used for a permanent place for the collection center. At its headquarters in New Haven, a place central for residents to travel to, a piece of the RWA's parking area was donated for the HazWaste facility. An amendment to the Land Use Plan was necessary as the area had been designated "Water Supplies Facilities" in the 1983 document. When the Representative Policy Board discussed the change to "Other Land Development", the representative from New Haven volunteered the information that the City had held public hearings on the subject and that no verbal opposition nor adverse correspondence had been presented.[126] One of the sticking points could have been that the city did not want suburban trash, an argument that had been advanced all too often when communities had attempted to get together to hold joint days. Few towns wanted to be recipients of household hazardous waste generated in another town. The RPB approved the amendment unanimously and RCOG appointed a HazWaste Central Municipal Planning Committee to work on budget and to develop policy.

Connecticut's first regional household hazardous waste collection center was opened by the RWA in March 1990. A building was constructed to house the facility and the costs associated with it were shared by the member towns and the state. A state license to operate the collection center was required. Bids were solicited. From the four finalists, Laidlaw Environmental Services (Northeast) Inc. of Andover, Massachusetts was selected to be the contractor to handle the waste for a period of five years. Laidlaw operated the facility with the help of volunteers from member towns. An annual operating and maintenance budget is developed by Darrell Smith, Director of the RWA Water Quality Division and the member towns are assessed a share of the disposal costs. The towns reimburse the RWA for expenses incurred. The HazWaste Central Municipal Planning Committee approves the budget. Towns belonging to the cooperative venture are Bethany, Branford, Cheshire, East Haven, Fairfield, Guilford,

Hamden, Lyme, Madison, Milford, New Haven, North Branford, North Haven, Orange, Prospect, Wallingford, West Haven, and Woodbridge.[127]

The success of the operation was immediate and is easily illustrated. In 1994, the center was opened for sixteen Saturdays and 4,046 users deposited gallons of waste oil and 490 drums of household hazardous waste in a facility capable of disposing of it properly, rather than having some portion of it wind up dumped illegally on the watershed. In addition, two satellite days were held that attracted another eight hundred residents of Lyme and Fairfield. The actual cost came to slightly over a quarter of a million dollars.[128] HazWaste Central is an outstanding example of regional cooperation.

In 1977, the mission of the Regional Water Authority was defined in the first section of its enabling legislation: first provide high quality drinking water and consistent with that, advance "the conservation and compatible recreational use of land held by the Authority". Former mayor of New Haven Frank Logue has said that when he started New Haven thinking about city ownership of the utility, one of his motives was "lust for the land...just think of all the recreational opportunities for the people of New Haven".[129] His sentiment is echoed by the Trust for Public Land in the statement: "Because it is sometimes dismissed as a frill, access to natural areas is a poor contender for limited public funds. But by large majorities, people who live in cities regard access to open space as among the most important factors in their well-being and the vitality of their neighborhoods."[130] New Haven's suburbs echoed both sentiments as the stimulus for regional ownership came largely from the desire for open space and recreational needs of the region.

Taking its legislative mandate most seriously, the RWA embarked on a recreation program to allow multiple use of watershed lands. During the drafting of the Land Use Plan, considerable emphasis was placed on opening up recreational opportunities for the public. Determining that whatever programs were offered would be on a fee/permit basis and that the state Department of Health would both by law and by desire have to approve of them, the RWA began eliciting public opinions regarding public need. Passive recreation, such as hiking, was a natural as miles of wood roads and trails already existed.

Fishing was contemplated on a trial program basis as a result of the East Haven Fishing Association's pressure to reopen Lake Saltonstall as it had been from the early 1990s until 1964.[131](see Appendix F) The Bethany Horsemen had an agreement with New Haven Water Company that they were most anxious to continue. Joggers, bird-watchers, cross country skiers, and nature lovers all were interested in having access to what had been, prior to public ownership, forbidden territory.

The programs resulting from both internal interest and public pressure made the RWA's recreation a model for other water utilities. Over fifty miles of trails are open for hiking, jogging, cross country skiing, and nature study. The horseback riding program, considered by many to be an elite sport for the very privileged, was expanded to include public events, plus the group was required to bear the costs and maintenance of the trails. Fishing is allowed on ten miles of rivers and streams as well as on Lake Saltonstall, Lake Chamberlain, and the Maltby Lakes. On Lake Saltonstall, there is a dock that allows physically challenged fishing enthusiasts to participate in catching supper; the first of its kind on a reservoir in Connecticut, it was funded by a grant from the U.S. Department of Education. DEP has responded to the fishing program by overseeing and stocking Lake Saltonstall, guaranteeing that the lake will not be fished out. Another wheelchair accessible fishing platform was constructed at Clark's Pond, in Hamden after the pond itself was restored in 1989.[132]

Combining the recreation program with an education program, self-guided nature trails have been created for Lake Saltonstall and Racebrook.[133] A grant was received for Racebrook from the U.S. Department of Education for a 2,000 foot wheelchair accessible inter-pretative nature trail and was the first such trail to be constructed by a Connecticut water utility. A handsomely illustrated guide written by the Manager of Education Rosemary Macionus is available for all those taking advantage of the trail. At Lake Saltonstall, the self-guided trail is a mile and a half long and "describes the role the woodlands play in protecting our water supply". Plants, animal life, the hydro-logic cycle, and forest management are described in greater detail in a booklet available to hikers.[134]

To suggest that all the recreation programs were put in place without some pushing and pulling would be naive. Parking lots had to be constructed, and residents near them often complained of increased traffic, noise and litter. In most cases, the apprehensions were relieved as experience demonstrated fishermen, hikers and nature lovers were respectful of neighborhoods as well as open space. In one instance, the RWA was willing to take a member town to court in order to keep a program going but the overwhelming enthusiasm for the recreational opportunities has had a calming effect on those detractors.

Originally, the fishing program at Lake Saltonstall had a boat and electric motor rental adjunct, but state law had to be changed in order for the program to continue, as only boats propelled by oars were allowed in order to protect drinking water quality. Another part of the program at Saltonstall allowed fishermen to bring their own boats and motors to the lake. At approximately the same time that the electric motors were okayed, the threat of zebra mussels, shellfish that reproduce rapidly, clogging pipes, was recognized and the RWA vetoed the use of privately owned boats and motors. Fishermen could no longer bring their own boats and motors.[135] Additionally, as summer progresses lake levels usually drop. The shallow side of Lake Saltonstall is the side where shore fishing is allowed, and as fewer people took advantage of the opportunity to fish, the hours were curtailed. On the whole people responded positively to the need to control expenses.

For the first ten years of operation the entire recreational program of the RWA required subsidies as high as $125,000. By 1995, the operation was largely self-supporting. Plans are underway to consider a trail for mountain bike use to be administered as the horseback riding program. Efforts continue to connect RWA trails with trails owned or administered by other entities, and with the new Greenway Initiative in Connecticut. Assuredly, there will be future chances for expanded activities.[136]

The most innovative venture that the RWA has embarked on is that of environmental education. The entrance of the utility into the world of dispensing knowledge has been exciting as the RWA has had to develop its own materials and curriculum as well as find space to carry out the program.

The genesis came from Otto Schaefer, the RWA's Senior

Advisor-Land and the mastermind of the Land Use Plan. During the developmental stages of the plan, Schaefer dreamed that the RWA could make use of its human and natural resources to bring to the public an educational program that would concentrate on water resources and water quality. He envisioned that at Lake Gaillard, the largest reservoir in the system and the one with such fragile soil that extensive recreation would be prohibited, would serve as an enormous outdoor classroom, with perhaps an interpretative kiosk or building that could house classrooms and exhibits. Realizing that financing could be a problem, partners were sought for the venture. Connecticut Audubon Society seemed a good fit with mission and motives similar to the RWA's and an agreement was concluded with the organization, but never implemented.[137]

Unwilling to give up, the RWA continued its quest for a suitable location and partner. Finally, to go forward alone became the wisest course. The nineteenth century operations building below the dam at Lake Whitney was available; it could house classrooms and offices. The reservoir and the Mill River were immediately at hand and right next door was the Whitney Museum, a not-for-profit entity with wide public acceptance. And so an 1880s office building became the Whitney Water Center, the showpiece of the RWA's education program.

Obviously to begin, there had to be a financial commitment through the RWA's budget process. The five member RWA was solidly behind the proposal and the RPB came on board quickly. In 1990, the Center opened for grades pre-kindergarten through eight. With a curriculum developed by Rosemary Macionus and with grants from businesses and foundations, thousands of school children have had hands-on experiences in water based projects. As the application for the Renew America grant states, "the Whitney Water Center represents the first synthesis of environmental science education, educational use of water utility lands and historic sites...The Center is the first such educational facility to be developed for the express purpose of educating area students and adults through study of water science issues. The central theme is the relationship between water quality, the watershed, and human activities in the watershed." In an urban setting and with state of the art equipment including video microscopy and computers, teachers and students from the inner city and area towns have taken full advantage of the Center. From October 1990 to June 1994, more than 27,000 students had enjoyed the Center's educational opportunities. Besides the free programs offered to district towns, there is a for fee after school program and a summer experience offered so that the Center is booked all day and all year round.[138]

With a teacher training program to go along with the on site classes, the whole system reaches out to a wide constituency. Held on Saturdays, with such titles as Fall Birding, Rock Bottom—Geology for Beginners, Groundwater Models, and Spring Wildflowers, it is hardly a surprise that the teachers' training is highly popular and that class limits have had to be imposed. Coupled with a teachers' manual and student workbooks, the training program rounds out the educational program.

Recognized for its excellence, the Whitney Water Center is the proud recipient of the National Environmental Achievement Award given by Renew America.

So if the story began "once upon a time", one could almost expect it to end "and they all lived happily ever after". The reactions that were predicted that would exist between the land towns and consumer towns are not yet evident. There have been few RWA land sales, and far and away the majority of land that has been sold is permanently dedicated open space. Land towns vote consistently conservatively on financial matters and consumer towns support subsidies for recreation and education. A successful regional project, HazWaste, has been developed under the aegis of the RWA and a model recreation program is in full operation.

Perhaps Thayer Baldwin's comment best defines the RWA: "It is a very, very, successful operation. It seems to run like a dream. The public interest is well represented".[139]

The South Central Connecticut Regional Water Authority is indeed an ongoing entity. It will fall on future historians to determine if there is a fairy tale ending, or any ending at all.

PART SIX

Aftermath: Lessons Learned from the New Haven Story

When the city of New Haven and its suburban towns reached accord on the ownership and management of New Haven Water Company, a partnership was formed. Hammering out agreements on the complexities of tax issues and multiple land uses for water supply and recreation, formed the basis for breaking down conventional barriers and recognizing regional solutions to meeting shared needs.

Today the debate over how to provide safe drinking water continues: over source protection as a viable alternative to filtration; over the role of regulation, incentives, and land acquisition in water supply source protection; over equitable distribution of the costs and benefits. What relevance does the New Haven experience have for water policy decision makers in 1996?

Across America, water companies are grappling with whether to filter or not to filter to meet federal Safe Drinking Water Act requirements.

Under the 1986 amendments, the filtration requirement may be waived if the water meets federal drinking water standards, provided an effective watershed protection program is in place to prevent water quality degradation. Filtration avoidance strategies are being developed as alternatives to the enormous costs of installing water treatment plants.

In the 1970s, New Haven Water Company selected a strategy not foreseen by the architects of the federal mandate. Faced with the expense of filtration plant construction, the Water Company chose to generate the needed capital by selling almost two-thirds of its watershed landholdings. The enormous public outcry to this policy decision was unanticipated and led to public acquisition of the investor-owned company.

Residents of the metropolitan towns, viewing the land as an integral part of their community character, providing them a sense of place and open space, vehemently opposed the proposed land sales. State health officials, viewing the watershed lands as essential for water supply source protection, urged greater restrictions on the land's use. The State Department of Environmental Protection assumed the water supply lands were dedicated open space, guiding regional growth and enabling opportunities for compatible recreation.

Realizing the critical link between the city and its water supply watershed, the city's mayor and several legislators introduced legislation imposing a moratorium on the land sales and proposing public ownership of the water works.

Belatedly recognizing the public's view that the value of water supply watershed as a significant natural and cultural resource was greater than its value as a market commodity, New Haven Water Company President Charles E. Woods "somewhat ruefully describe[d] the company's land-sale announcement as a major error in public relations".[140]

More than a public relations error, it was a fatal misjudgement of wise land use. It became an example for other water companies of how *not* to meet the federal mandate.

Public acquisition of New Haven Water Company expanded its focus of water supply management from the collection and delivery of clean water to encompass broader functions of the watershed and the concerns of the people living and working within it. The RWA enabling legislation, incorporated land classification standards for source protection, provisions for public recreation, and consideration of the financial impact upon ratepayers. Public participation became an integral part of the process of preparing RWA Land Use Plans. In addition, consistency with municipal, regional, and state land use plans was required by RWA land disposition policies. Although RWA has sold 1,125 acres since 1980, all but 109 acres have been for open space uses.

The RWA's expanded management planning provided a preview of the 1990s approaches to water resource management. Today, water*supply* management is increasingly becoming water*shed* management with plans reflecting the importance of partnerships with its residents. Conflict resolution has become an essential skill for today's watershed managers.

Analyzing New York City's struggle with upstate Catskill residents over watershed use, Yale University School of Forestry and Environmental Studies Ph.D. candidate Krystyna Stave observes, "On the surface . . . is a disagreement over how to prevent environmental degradation. At its core, however, the conflict involves a complex set of issues including politics from the local to the federal level, challenges to a rural lifestyle, distribution of the costs and benefits of resource protection and ecological processes that connect one resource with another."[141]

New York Governor George E. Pataki has taken the position he would "do whatever it takes to avoid filtration" from working with farmers and businesses on mutually beneficial voluntary programs to buying up to 80,000 acres from willing sellers to protect New York City's drinking water—the nation's largest unfiltered water*supply*.[142]

Watershed land acquisition is also the focus of filtration avoidance strategies of other major American cities. Although Boston Metropolitan District Commission's Quabbin Reservoir has met the Safe Drinking Water Act's criteria as an unfiltered water supply source, the Wachusett Reservoir has not. A recently approved $399,000,000 state open space bond includes funds for land acquisition in Wachusett's watershed.

New Jersey Governor Christine Todd Whitman has committed to a "hands across the border" $10,000,000 contribution toward purchasing the development-threatened New York portion of the metropolitan watershed in Sterling Forest from its Swiss owner, who is planning commercial recreation and housing development there.[143] The private non-profit Trust for Public Land and the Open Space Institute are negotiating the purchase on behalf of the two states.[144] Acknowledging the essential function that undeveloped land serves in preventing contaminants from reaching water supplies is long overdue. But is watershed source protection alone a viable alternative to filtration?

Connecticut's 1970s watershed land classification criteria are based upon the ability of soil to function as a natural filtration mechanism. However, New Haven's drinking water is also treated by filtration plants.

In North Carolina, where all surface water supplies are already filtered, state legislation requires local water authorities to develop watershed land use plans which must be approved by the state. Although such legislation can reduce the health risks of watershed development and the cost of water treatment, it cannot prevent future development.

To address the issue of source protection vs. filtration, the federal Environmental Protection Agency, in 1993, convened an expert panel chaired by University of North Carolina engineering professor Daniel A. Okun. Its findings called for New York City to filter its drinking water. This was unwelcome news to the City which refuted the report and to state and federal officials who ignored it.[145]

Consequently, Professor Okun brought his findings directly to the public, including a letter to the editor of *The New York Times* on May 28, 1994: "The assumption that watershed protection or filtration would be adequate is faulty. Almost all professionals agree that where substantial development has occurred on a watershed, as in New York, watershed protection and filtration are both necessary."

Recent outbreaks of illness, such as that caused by cryptosporidium in Milwaukee, have increased public demand for strengthened federal regulations governing the worst waterborne contaminants. However, unless the risks are reasonably defined, the costs of guarding against every possible pollutant are prohibitive. Providing both source protection and filtration is a cost effective approach to ensuring safe drinking water.

Successfully bucking the trend toward privatization, the RWA demonstrated that regional resource sharing is the most viable way of meeting the needs of the city and its suburbs.

One of the most difficult obstacles to overcome in passing the RWA enabling legislation taxation. Connecticut's reliance on the property tax exacerbated the difficulties. Towns counted on the large tax bills of New Haven Water Company based on ownership of vehicles, land and buildings, improvements such as dams and pumping stations, pipe and filter plants. With projected capital investments in excess of $100,000,000 towns looked forward to vastly increased revenues from the utility. New Haven, with the majority of consumers, was unwilling to have rates raised unreasonably as a result of increases to the grand lists. North Branford, where the filter plant for the largest reservoir was to be constructed in the 1980s, looked ahead to increased revenue to offset the cost of sewers. Other towns fell in between.

As the debate went on between city and suburb, the conflict was resolved with the embrace of the principle that there would be no erosion of the tax base with the regionalization of the water utility. Each town would receive payments based on the grand list on the date of acquisition. Payments would rise and fall with future assessments, but no new projects would be added to the list. Payments In Lieu Of Taxes represented equity to the member communities of the South Central Connecticut Regional Water Authority.

Protecting the water supply is the primary focus of all RWA land use policies. The household hazardous waste center, HazWaste, at RWA headquarters in New Haven, is owned and operated by the water utility, acting for the Regional Council of Governments. The regional center was formed to prevent hazardous substances from being improperly discarded, thereby contaminating the environment, including the drinking water supply.

Working together to solve the problem of environmental degradation, the towns had the vision of lower costs for the collection of hazardous waste materials and the RWA saw a way to effect a more efficient way to provide a necessary service. The initiative to go beyond single municipality waste collection days came from cost analysis, sound science, and a willingness to cooperate to accomplish something for the public benefit.

Watershed management and source protection cannot be conducted on a town by town basis as the watersheds do not respect town lines. The RWA has an active program for policing the watersheds and the program is reinforced with a center for educating future consumers on water supply protection by giving them an appreciation for a clean environment.

The Whitney Water Center teaches children the basics of drinking water science. It emphasizes the interdependency of source protection and safe drinking water. Thousands of students attend classes at the base of the dam at Lake Whitney annually to learn first hand about water science and drinking water, to learn about environmental issues that may conflict with safe drinking water, and to learn that we are all responsible for the quality of our drinking water.

The costs of the Whitney Water Center are borne by the ratepayer. Although grants and gifts have been received to offset some of these costs, the benefit of the center to the region has been evaluated and it has been determined that underwriting the program is in the best interests of the utility and the region.

The mission of the RWA mandated the recreational use of the 25,000 plus acres held at the time of acquisition. In drafting the Land Use Plan, public input was solicited to determine whether the expectations of the users would conform to the watershed management plans of the RWA. Many types of active recreation would have been unsuitable for water supply lands. Fortunately, hiking and fishing were the two activities most popular and with careful oversight could be conducted without threatening water quality.

In order to open the lands for passive recreation, parking lots had to be built, trails had to be identified and marked, a permit system had to be designed and marketed, and rules and regulations had to be formulated. Costs associated with the recreation program were high in the early years.

While the goal was to make recreation self supporting, the RWA made a policy decision that the mission of the institution called for subsidizing the program. In the beginning, $150,000 a year was necessary to make up the difference between permit sales and costs. Over time, the costs have come down and permit sales have gone up, so that an annual expenditure of $5,000 now covers the deficits.

Faithful to its mission of providing pure water at a reasonable cost and allowing recreational use of some of the largest tracts of the region's open space, the regional entity continually weighs public benefit against public costs.

Primary among the lessons to be learned from the New Haven experience is that illustrated by New Haven Water Company's ill-advised land sale proposal: the value of water supply watershed as a natural and human resource is far greater than its value as a market commodity—a message foretold by Frederick Law Olmstead in 1910. Management of the watershed's natural resource potential must extend beyond the collection and distribution of water to the activity and land use of the people who live within the watershed.

Although both source protection and filtration are necessary for safe drinking water, limiting watershed land activities to low risk uses minimizes the water treatment costs required.

Regional cooperation need not begin and end with water. Developing partnerships between cities and their suburbs for tax-sharing, recreation, hazardous waste collection and education recognizes that the economic and ecological concerns of residents in a metropolitan area are interdependent.

ENDNOTES

PART ONE - Reasons for Going Public

1. Jan Oscherwitz, "The History of the New Haven Water Company: Redefining Public Need", (senior essay, Yale University, 1984) 13.

2. Ibid., 15.

3. *Contract Between the City of New Haven and the New Haven Water Company*, 17 February 1902.

4. "Killian Raps Water Co. for Land Sale Proposal", *New Haven Register*, 26 April 1974.

5. "Lufkin Vows Fight Against Land Sale", *Hartford Courant*, 12 January 1974.

6. Private law passed in 1849, *An Act Incorporating The New Haven Water Company, Resolves and Private Laws of the State of Conn.* (1836-1856), 4:1369. Note: see also Code of City of New Haven, Conn.,Vol. 2, *Special Laws and General Ordinances, Title 2 Special Laws*, (Tallahasse, Fla. Municipal Code Corp., 1962), Sec. 111.

7. *Conn. Joint Standing Committee Hearings*, Environment, Pt. 4, 26 February, 10 March, 18 March 1977. (hereafter cited as *Conn. Comm. Hearings*).

8. *Christian Science Monitor*, 11 April 1977.

9. Richard S. Woodhull, Letter to Woods, 13 September 1976.

10. *Conn. Comm. Hearings*, Environment, Pt. 1, 18 March 1975.

11. Ibid.

12. Bridgeport Hydraulic Company v. Council on Water Company Lands, 453 Supp. 942 (D.Conn. 1977) aff'd. 439 U. S. 999 (1978).

13. *Report of the Connecticut Council on Water Company Lands*, February 1977, 8-11.

14. Governor Ella T. Grasso, Letter to Sen. James J. Murphy, Jr. and Rep. John W. Anderson, 8 March 1977.

15. *Report of the Commission to Study the Feasibility of a South Central Connecticut Regional Water District*, 5 January 1977, 1, 15. (hereafter cited as FSC Report).

16. John Crawford, Letter to Bennitt, 17 October 1994.

17. *FSC Report*, 5 January 1977, 16.

18. "Water Co. Cost Splits Aldermen", *New Haven Register*, 9 November 1977.

19. "Joint Quarry-Lake Plan Mapped in North Branford", *New Haven Register*, 13 July 1973.

20. Greenwich water company, et al. v. Howard E. Hausman. (J. D. Hartford/New Britain, Docket No. 10838, May 12, 1979) cert. denied 178 Conn. 755 (1974).

21. "Water Co. President May Profit by Sale", *Journal-Courier* 5 April 1978. Note: Third of five feature articles by Andrew L. Houlding.

22. "Cohn To Realize Profit From Stock", *Journal-Courier*, 8 April 1978. Note: Fourth of five articles by Andrew L. Houlding. Mr. Cohn also was campaign treasurer for Mayor Logue's 1977 reelection campaign at the time Logue was pushing for public purchase of the utility.

23. Charles E. Woods, "Utility Company Lands", *Connecticut Woodlands*, Spring 1974, 7, 8.

24. *FSC Report*, 9.

25. Ibid., 31.

26. Ibid., 32.

27. *FSC Report Executive Summary*, 5 January 1977, 3.

28. *New Haven Register*, 13 April 1966.

29. "Hearing Scheduled on Regional Water Plan", *New Haven Register*, 5 February 1977.

PART TWO - Legislative History of South Central Connecticut Regional Water Authority

30. "Time and Water Company Land", *New Haven Register*, 5 December 1974.

31. Conn. Public Acts, 75-405 *An Act Concerning the Sale of Water Company Lands.*

32. Ibid., 77-606 *An Act Concerning the Council on Water Company Lands.*

33. Conn. Gen. Assembly, HB7669 *An Act Concerning the Study of the Creation of a Regional of a Regional Water Authority for the New Haven Region*, 1975.

34. Ibid., SB504 *An Act Authorizing the City of New Haven Purchase or Condemn the New Haven Water Company and Operate a Regional Water System*, 1976. Note: Subsequently, because only the House members of the committee approved SB504, it became listed as SHB5691.

35. "Area Towns Rap Water Co. Sale Bill", *New Haven Register*, 28 March 1976.

36. "Water Co. Measure Remains in Limbo", *New Haven Register*, 12 March 1976.

37. *Conn. Comm. Hearings*, Regulated Activities and Energy, Pt.1, 25 March 1976, 6-25, 39-40.

38. "Water Co. Talks Wednesday", *New Haven Register*, 30 March 1976.

39. Note: For further discussion of this proposal see also "Public Ownership of Water Co. Proposed", *New Haven Register*, 12 October 1975, and "Alternative Plan Eyed for Water Co.", *New Haven Register,* 8 March 1976.

40. See note 5.

41. "Suburbs Seek Study on Regional Water Authority", *New Haven Register*, 1 April 1976. Note: When Bennitt interviewed Mayor Logue in his home in New Haven on 28 October 1994, he pointed out that he learned about the 1902 option from Joel Cohn in 1974, and had been urging this action since then. At that time Logue had the New Haven Board of Aldermen appoint a special committee

to look into exercising the option.

42. "Water Co. Briefs Its Shareholders", *New Haven Register*, 6 April 1976.

43. New Haven Water Co., *Minutes,* Board of Directors, 11 February 1976.

44. Howard D. Brooks, Remarks to the Representative Policy Board of the RWA, 16 January 1992.

45. Ibid. SA 77-98 provides for Payments In Lieu of Taxes (PILOT) by the RWA to each community in the water district. PILOT is to be paid on land and improvements as of the date of acquisition of the Water Company. Improvements, such as filtration plants, made following acquistion are specifically excluded from PILOT, except for pipe laid in the ground. Payments are based on the towns' evaluations and mill rates, which fluctuate over time. The theory behind PILOT is that there should be no erosion of the tax base.

46. *FSC Report*, 5 January 1977, 31.

47. Ibid., 4,5,6.

48. Charles E. Woods, Letter to McCluskey, 25 September 1974. See also "Mrs. McCluskey Hits McKosky Water Land Stand", *Journal Courier* 24 September 1974.

49. Conn. Gen. Assembly, HB5995, 1977.

50. Conn. Comm. Hearings, Regulated Activities and Energy, Pt. 14, 1977.

51. Ibid., 58. Note: In a telephone interview with McCluskey on 16 November 1994, Thayer Baldwin informed her he had talked frequently with Rep. George Ritter about regional ownership. Rep. Ritter "understood the problems of the city". Baldwin described the condemnation bill as "a city incentive to have others take them seriously". The city of New Haven's *objective* was public ownership, but its *preference* was regional ownership.

52. Ibid.

53. Ibid., 18.

54. Ibid., Regulated Activities and Energy and Environment, Part 1, 1977.

55. Conn. Gen. Assembly, 20 *House of Representative Proceedings*, Part 16, 1977, 6538.

56. Ibid., 6563.

57. Ibid., 6556, 6557.

58. Harry J. Wexler, Memo to Feasibility Study Commission, 17 June 1977.

59. *Conn. Special Acts*, 1977, 2:111.

60. "Dire Results of Grasso Veto", *New Haven Register*, 17 July 1977.

61. B. Patrick Madden, Letter to Gov. Ella T. Grasso, 19 July 1977.

62. Jay W. Jackson, Memo to Gov. Ella T. Grasso, 19 July 1977.

63. Rep. McCluskey, Rep. Stevens and Sen. Madden, memo to Members of the General Assembly, 20 July 1977.

64. Conn. Gen. Assembly, *20 House of Representatives Proceedings, Part 16, 1977 Special Session*, 25 July 1977, 6925.

65. Ibid., 6929.

66. Howard D. Brooks, Memo to McCluskey, 22 July 1977.

67. Conn. Gen. Assembly, *20 House of Representaatives Proceedings, Part 16, 1977 Special Session*, 6939.

68. Ibid., *20 Senate Proceedings, Part 10, 1977 Special Session*, 4299.

69. Ibid. 4317

70. Conn. Special Acts, 1977.

PART THREE - Acquisition: What is a Fair Purchase Price

71. Thayer Baldwin disclosed to McCluskey in a telephone interview in November 1944 that the city had hired R.W. Beck Associates to perform an engineering survey of New Haven Water Company "to show serious intent to purchase and to obtain hard based data for subsequent discussions".

72. South Central Connecticut Regional Water Authority, *Minutes*, 8 December 1977.

73. City of New Haven, *Minutes*, Board of Aldermen, 8 December 1977.

74. Mayor Frank Logue, *Testimony* to Board of Aldermen, 8 December 1977.

75. New Haven Water Company, *Minutes*, Board of Directors, 14 November 1977.

76. Charles E. Woods, Letter to Howard D. Brooks, 18 October 1977.

77. South Central Connecticut Regional Water Authority, *Acquisition Plan*, 28 December 1977.

78. *New Haven Register*, 2 January 1974.

79. *New Haven Register*, 28 January 1978.

80. South Central Connecticut Regional Water Authority, *Acquisition Plan*, 28 December 1977.

81. South Central Connecticut Regional Water Authority *Minutes*, 11 December 1977.

82. South Central Connecticut Regional Water Authority *Minutes*, 11 January 1978

83. New Haven Water Company *Minutes*, Board of Directors, 11 February 1978.

84. City of New Haven, *Minutes*, Board of Aldermen, 14 April 1978.

85. South Central Connecticut Regional Water Authority, *Minutes*, 12 February 1978.

86. New Haven Water Company, *Minutes of Annual Meeting*, 17   April 1978.

87. South Central Connecticut Regional Water Authority-New Haven Board of Aldermen, *Agreement*, 21 June 1978.

88. City of New Haven, *Minutes*, Board of Aldermen, 26 June 1978

89. South Central Connecticut Regional Water Authority, *Minutes*, 30 November 1978.

90. *New Haven Register*, 9 January 1979.

91. *New Haven Register*, 21 December 1978.

92. *New Haven Register*, 5 January 1979.

93. Thayer Baldwin, Jr., Letter to Howard Brooks, 14 January 1979. Joel Cohn, owner of the largest single chunk of water company stock, was a prime mover behind public ownership. In a telephone interview with McCluskey on 16 November 1994, Baldwin described Cohn as an entrepreneur — "a gnat in the hair of the Water Company Board"— who bought into the Water Company with the expectation of profits from the vastly increased value of the land. "He realized sooner than Water Company management

that it wasn't going to work"—the chance for windfall land sale profits was on a collision course with the current state and regulatory climate. What would work was the sale of Water Company assets at an attactive price rather than waiting for legislative restrictions.

Cohn's efforts to wake up the Water Company, long accustomed to silent shareholders, "to the realities of the work and give the shareholders a significant return on their investment" led to his being dumped from the Board in April 1974. He was the first Director in the Company's 72 year history whose request for renomination had been turned down. Subsequent Board negotations focusing on maximum returns to shareholders led to an internal struggle culminating in the 1979 formation of the Alternate Slate of Directors. Note: see also *New Haven Register* 20 April 1979.

94. South Central Connecticut Regional Water Authority, *Minutes*, 3 July 1979.

95. *New Haven Register*, 28 April 1978

96. South Central Connecticut Regional Water Authority, *Minutes*, 3 July 1979.

97. The town of Wallingford had negotiated with NHWC for the purchase of 753 acres. Unable to reach agreement, Wallingford condemned the property and left it to the court to determine the price. Wallingford remained the seventeenth member of the water district through 1980, after which the town was removed from the roll as there were neither water customers nor land owned by the RWA within its boundaries.

98. New Haven Water Company, *Minutes*, Board of Directors, 8 August 1979.

99. South Central Connecticut Regional Water Authority, *Minutes*, 5 October 1979.

100. The comment was made by Michael Reddy of Morgan Guaranty Trust Company.

101. New Haven Water Company, *Minutes*, Board of Directors, 4 December 1979.

102. *New Haven Register*, 22 February 1979.

103. The reverse merger was used to avoid a tax assessment by the Internal Revenue Service, a move which would have eroded the stockholders' share of the $93 per share offering.

104. South Central Connecticut Regional Water Authority, *Agreement and Plan of Merger*, 7 March 1980.

105. South Central Connecticut Regional Water Authority, *Minutes*, 5 April 1980.

106. South Central Connecticut Regional Water Authorioty, *Bond Resolution*, 31 July 1980.

107. New Haven Water Company, *Minutes of Annual Meeting*, 20 May 1980.

108. South Central Connecticut Regional Water Authority, *Official Statement*, 8 August 1980.

109. Ibid.

PART FOUR - The Changing of the Guard

110. *Journal Courier*, 24 June 1981.

111. *New Haven Register*, 28 June 1981.

112. South Central Connecticut Regional Water Authority, *Minutes*, October 1980.

113. *New Haven Register*, 17 May 1980.

114. South Central Connecticut Regional Water Authority, *Official Statement*, 1980, p.8.

115. South Central Connecticut Regional Water Authority, *Land Use Plan*, 1983, p.4.

116. Ibid.

117. Ibid. p.V.

118. Bennitt had been concerned that the provisions of SA 77-98 would not prevail in cases of land sales. She requested that Otto Schaefer obtain a legal opinion upholding Section 18 of the RWA enabling legislation. In a July 10, 1981 Memorandum to Richard McHugh, Schaefer affirmed that SA 77-98 was upheld by legal counsel.

119. Richard McHugh, Otto Schaefer, Correspondence and Memorandum on sale of Wintergreen land, 1983.

120. South Central Connecticut Regional Water Authority, *Land Use Plan - 1993 Update*, appendix C. Table 2. On February 24, 1994 the RWA adopted an updated Land Use Plan and submitted it to the RPB for approval. The Plan was rejected because the RPB

believed that it did not have sufficient emphasis on land conservation and that significant land sales would occur. On April 18, 1996 the RPB approved the December 14, 1995 *Land Use Plan -1995 update* with only Orange and Woodbridge voting against it. The new Plan calls for conservation of all RWA land holdings with the exception of 96 acres most of which were previously approved for sale by the RPB. In addition the 1995 Plan seeks to find ways to offset the cost to the ratepayers for conservation.

PART FIVE - The Sleepy Old Water Company as a Vibrant Agendy

121. Matt Bai et al. "Does New York Have a Drinking Problem?", *New York,* 16 January 1995, p. 26.

122. *New York Times*, Editorial, 12 December 1994.

123. *American City and Country*, Volume 110, No. 2, February 1995, p.56.

124. Peter Rogers, *America's Water: Federal Roles and Responsibilities, A Twentieth Century Fund Book*, 1993, p.48.

125. A complete review of internal memoranda and documents of the Land Management Division of the Regional Water Authority provided details for the aquifer protection information. In addition several interviews were held with Thomas Chaplik and Otto Schaefer by Bennitt.

126. South Central Connecticut Regional Water Authority, *Minutes*, RPB meeting 12 December 1989.

127. Details on the HazWaste Center were provided in interviews with Thomas Barger and Darrell Smith conducted by Bennitt.

128. Thomas Barger, Interview with Bennitt, 2 October 1995.

129. Frank Logue, Interview with Bennitt, 7 November 1995.

130. Trust for Public Land, *Healing America's Cities*, 1995, p.13.

131. Otto Schaefer, Interview, with Bennitt, 9 October 1995.

132. South Central Connecticut Regional Water Authority, *Land Use Plan - 1993 Update*, p.10.

133. Rosemary Macionus, Interview with Bennitt, 2 October 1994.

134. South Central Connecticut Regional Water Authority,

Lake Saltonstall Native Trail *Guide.*

135. John Hudak, Interview with Bennitt, 2 October 1994.

136. Otto Schaefer, Interview with Bennitt, 2 October 1994.

137. Ibid.

138. Kathleen Powell, Interview with Bennitt, 16 November 1994.

139. Thayer Baldwin, Jr., Interview with McCluskey, 16 November 1994.

PART SIX - Aftermath: Lessons Learned from the New Haven Story

140. Andrew L. Houlding, *New Haven Register*, Fourth of a series of five articles, 8 April 1978.

141. Krystyna A. Stave, "Resource Conflict in New York City's Catskill Watersheds: A Case for Expanding The Scope of Water Resource Management", American Water Resources Association conference presentation, April 1995: 3.

142. *New York Times*, Editorial, 16 January 1995.

143. *New York Times,* Editorial, 29 September 1995.

144. The Trust For Public Land, "Watershed Protection Has Mainstream Appeal", *Green Sense: Financing Parks and Conservation*, vol. 2, no. 1. Spring 1996.

145. Matt Bai et al., "Does New York Have A Drinking Problem?", *New York,*. 16 January 1995: 29.

Acknowledgements

We are deeply indebted to Donald B. Hyatt, whose editorial skill and enthusiastic support for the venture *Who Wants to Buy a Water Company?* gave the authors courage and stamina.

We are very grateful to the Regional Water Authority for authorizing and supporting the project as well as providing open access for the necessary research.

Many others were helpful in the preparation of the manuscript. John J. Crawford, Thayer Baldwin, Jr., Frank Logue, G. Harold Welch, Jr., and Russell Brenneman read the text and provided their expert guidance. Thomas Jackson contributed advice and advocacy. Jeanne H. Hyatt researched, typed, and collated—all done with grace and a smile.

Appendix A

THE PLAYERS

New Haven Water Company 1977:

Board of Directors: Mary Arnstein, Paul Johnson, William Lyons, John McDevitt, Gerald Fellows, Arthur Sachs, Norman Botwinik, John Embersits, H. Everton Hosley, C. Raymond Brock, William Gumbart, Allen Carmichael, Donald Keefe.

Management: Charles E. Woods, President; John J. Crawford, Executive Vice President; Richard McHugh, Vice President for Engineering; Marshall Chiaraluce, Secretary.

Tyler, Cooper, Grant, Bowerman and Keefe:

Donald Keefe, Corporation Counsel for New Haven Water Company, on Board of Directors

Joseph Cohn and Son:

Joel Cohn, father of Betsy Henley-Cohn, New Haven Water Company Board member until 1974, replaced by Thayer Baldwin, Jr.

Holt, Wexler and Associates, consultants

Harry J. Wexler, Philetus H. Holt

First Representative Policy Board:

Howard D. Brooks, Chair, Nicholas Amodio, John M. C. Betts, Frederick Chase, Stephen Darley, Leonard Johnson, William Knight, Elizabeth Lapham, Fred Mauger, Vincent Mascia, Donald S. McCluskey, Edward Measom, Raymond Puslys, George Sago, Russell Stoddard, Eric Stone, and James Varrone

First Regional Water Authority:

Claire C. Bennitt, John M. C. Betts, Howard D. Brooks, Joseph A. Cermola, G. Harold Welch, Jr. Staff: Jeanne H. Hyatt

Governor's Office:

Ella T. Grasso, Governor; Jay Jackson, Counsel; Robert Killian, Lieutenant Governor.

City of New Haven:

Frank Logue, Mayor 1976-79; Thayer Baldwin, Jr., City Corporation Counsel and former director of New Haven Water Company (4/74-2/76); Albert Landino, Administrator of

Economic Development and a key player in the Democratic Administration; Judith Baldwin, Majority Leader of Board of Aldermen and wife of Thayer Baldwin.

1975 Aldermanic Special Water Company Study Committee appointed by Mayor Logue:

John Daniels, Judith Baldwin, Arthur DeSorbo, Charles Malick, Jr., Vincent Mauro, President Board of Aldermen, Consultant: R. W. Beck Associates, Jeffrey Clunie, Thomas Huse.

July 1977 Negotiating Team appointed by Mayor Logue:

Albert Landino; Leon Spencer and Jeffrey Clunie of R. W. Beck; Board of Aldermen Advisory Group Vincent Mauro, John Daniels, Arthur DeSorbo, Thayer Baldwin , Jr., Rosa DeLauro, Mayor's Executive Assistant

North Branford:

Timothy Ryan, Mayor; Pasquale Young, Deputy Mayor; Town Council

Council on Water Company Lands:

Sarah W. Richards, Chair

Regional Council of Elected Officials:

Robert Johnson, Mayor of West Haven, Chairman 1977; Norris Andrews, Executive Director.

Murtha, Cullina, Richter and Pinney:

Russell L. Brenneman, Esq., former Counsel of Department of Environmental Protection

Regional Water Authority Acquisition Team:

Hawkins, Delafield and Wood, Richard Sigal; Goldman Sachs, Stuart Fuchs; Morgan Guaranty Trust Company, Perry Hall, Charles Gruye, Howard (Sandy) Curlett, Michael Reddy, Alan Anders; Coopers and Lybrand, Martin Abrahams; Day, Berry and Howard, Isaac Russell, Daniel Anthony, Martin Budd, and Edward See.

Alternate Slate Opposing New Haven Water Company Board 1979:

Led by Betsy Henley-Cohn, daughter of Joel Cohn, Thayer Baldwin, Jr., Water Company Director 1974-1976, Moishe Reiss, Stanley N. Bergman, Harvey L. Koizim, Bertrand L. McTeague, Tracey J. Stangle, Orville Tice, James Tobin, Pasquale Young and Mario J. Zangari.

South Central Connecticut Regional Water Authority Management 1980:
Charles E. Woods, CEO; Marshall Chiaraluce, Director of
Administration; Richard McHugh, Director of Engineering;
Gerald McCann, Director of Finance; Donald Jackson, Director
of Operations; Otto E. Schaefer, Land Manager.
Consumer Counsel for Regional Water District:
David S. Silverstone, Esquire, Silverstone and Koontz

Appendix B

CHRONOLOGY

WATER COMPANY LAND SALES

1849   The CT General Assembly grants a private charter incorporating New Haven Water Company (NHWC) for the purpose of supplying the City of New Haven with pure water for public and domestic use.

2/17/02 A renegotiated contract provides for a City purchase option every 25 years, free water for municipal purposes, fixed rates for consumers, and construction of a filtration plant on Lake Whitney.

1967   Public Act 67-577 gives towns first refusal over water company land sales, with 45 days to state intent, 60 days to acquire.

3/25/70 New Haven Mayor Guida suggests Regional Council of Elected Officials (RCEO) study the feasibility of purchasing NHWC to avoid constant rate increases.

4/22/70 Woods tells RCEO that purchase of the Water Company by area towns could result in increased rates for consumers.

2/2/71   NHWC proposes creating a holding company with a subsidiary Eli Whitney Development Corporation (letter to stockholders).

3/10/71 NHWC announces plans to build a $15,000,000 filtration plant in North Branford and a $4,500,000 plant in East Haven.

1972   Public Act 721-189, the Uniform Accounting Procedures Act, PUC regulations require land sales profits to go to the ratepayer rather than the stockholder. NHWC and the

American Water Works Association challenge the regulation. The PUC regulation is upheld, <u>Greenwich Water Company et. al. v. Howard Hausman</u>, (J.D. Hartford/New Britain, Docket No 10838, May 12, 1979) <u>cert. denied,</u> 178 Conn. 755 (1979).

1972   Public Act 72-189 adds state right of first refusal of water company land sales.

1/2/74   NHWC announces plan to sell 16,000 acres.

4/74   Director Joel Cohn is dumped from the NHWC Board—the first director in the company's 72 year history whose request for renomination was turned down.

1974/75   Regional Committee on NHWC land sale study formed by RCEO.

1975   Public Act 75-405 imposes a two year moratorium on sale of water company land, creates a Council on Water Company Lands to inventory and study the disposition of such land and extends the time for municipalities first refusal from 90 days to 18 months.

7/7/75   Bridgeport Hydraulic Company challenges the constitutionality of the moratorium.

10/12/75   Environmental Protection Association of South Central Connecticut proposes a plan for public ownership of NHWC.

3/76   NHWC contract with Holt, Wexler and Associates to explore public ownership.

12/76   Yale Task Force on Water Company Lands.

2/77   Council on Water Company Lands submits Report to the General Assembly.

6/8/77   Public Act 77-606 establishes a water company lands classification system and extends the moratorium on Class II land sales for two years or until the Department of Health regulations to implement it are passed.

1977   Public Act 77-98 *An Act Concerning Financial Assistance for Water Companies for Construction of Treatment Facilities and Creating A South Central Connecticut Regional Water Authority* passes

12/29/77 U.S. District Court upholds moratorium on water company land sales and the state's right to restrict water company land sales in order to protect public health—<u>Bridgeport Hydraulic Co. vs Council on Water Company Lands of the State of Connecticut</u> 453 F. Supp. 942 (D. Conn. 1977) <u>aff'd</u>. 439 U.S. 999 (1978)

10/19/78 NHWC opposes State Health Department regulations classifying watershed lands and limiting sales.

2/6/80   General Assembly Regulations Review Committee approves regulations classifying water company land. Regulations of Connecticut State Agencies Sec.25-37c-1 through 25-32d-9.

LEGISLATION

1/75   Reps. McCluskey and Grasser introduce HB7669 *An Act Concerning the Creation of A Regional Water Authority for the New Haven Region.*

3/8/76   Regulated Activities and Energy Committeee (RAE) holds hearing on SB504 *An Act Authorizing the City of New Haven To Purchase of Condemn the New Haven Water Company and Operate A Regionnal Water System.*

3/10/76 RAE Committee votes favorably on SB504 after renumbering it to SHB5691.

3/25/76 RAE Committee holds hearing in North Branford on SHB5691. Rep. McCluskey proposes bill be amended to create a regional water authority.

3/31/76 RCEO approves proposing a regional water authority feasibility study bill.

4/6/76 House agrees to introduce a regional water authority feasibility study bill as an amendment to the City of New Haven condemnation bill SHB5691.

4/15/76 House passes SHB5691 with vote of 134-7.

5/76 Senate passes SHB5691, Special Act 76-68 *A Commission to Study the Feasibility of A South Central Connecticut Regional Water District.*

1/5/77 Feasibility Study Commission submits Report to the General Assembly. Reps. McCluskey and Stevens and Sen. Leiberman introduce HB5995 *An Act Establishing SCCRWA.*

2/14/77 RAE Committee holds hearing in North Branford on HB5995.

2/20/77 City of New Haven's option to purchase NHWC matures and is extended for six months, then three months to 11/20/77 cannot be further extended.

2/25/77 *RAE/Environment Committees* joint hearing at State Capitol on HB5995.

4/6/77 Rep. McCluskey submits HB5995 amendments to RAE Committee.

4/7/77 RAE Committee votes favorably to send SHB5995 to Appropriations Committee- Vote 8-1.

4/20/77 RCEO agrees upon recommended amendments to HB5995 but fails to act in time to meet Committee deadline of 4/3/77.

5/23/77 Senate petitions SHB5995 (file no.1117) from *Appropriations Committee.*

6/2/77 Senate President Killian, referring to a ruling on the Bottle Bill, rules that the Senate lacks authority to petition a House bill. Therefore SHB5995 is recommitted, effectively killing it.

6/7/77 House passes HB7958, file no. 1213, *An Act Concerning Financial Assistance For Water Companies For Construction of Treatment Facilities With Amendment A* (LCO 887), which is basically the same bill as SHB5995 and Amendment B, which tightens bond issuing procedures.

6/8/77 Senate passes HB7958, as amended by House Amendments and B.

7/14/77 Governor Grasso vetoes SHB7958, Special Act 77-98.

7/20/77 Meeting of New Haven area legislators with Governor Grasso to discuss adverse impact of veto.

7/25/77 House overrides Governor Grasso's veto of Special Act 77-98 by a VOTE of 116-23. Senate overrides veto by VOTE of 27-5.

ACQUISITION

12/8/77 At a New Haven Board of Aldermen's public hearing, suburban towns oppose City acquisition of the Water Company urging the Board to endorse regional ownership.

12/28/77 RWA approves acquisition plan at a price of $76 per share. Sixty percent of towns must ratify.

1/19/78 NHWC Board of Directors rejects RWA offer.

2/20/78 New Haven Board of Aldermen approves acquisition offer of $110,000,000 (or $84 per share).

4/78   Special Act 78-24 *An Act Concerning the South Central Connecticut Regional Water Authority* amends Special Act 77-98 preventing expansion of the water district without approval of the General Assembly and providing for an appointee of the Governor to serve on the Representative Policy Board.

4/5/78 Rep. McCluskey charges that the NHWC's advice to their shareholders that they would profit more by selling excess land than by accepting a RWA purchase offer ignores state restrictions on water company land sales.

4/17/78 NHWC shareholders reject RWA $76 per share purchase offer.

6/26/78 New Haven Board of Aldermen approve purchase offer of $102,000,000 and will assign the purchase agreement to RWA.

12/13/78 NHWC Board of Directors reject City's $110,000,000 purchase offer.

12/21/78 In a *New Haven Register* Op Ed article, Rep. McCluskey criticizes NHWC for rejecting "three generous purchase offers" by the RWA.

1/5/79 NHWC responds to Rep. McCluskey with a full page ad in the *New Haven Register* entitled "Who Is It That's Misleading the Public?"

5/24/79 NHWC shareholders defeat "Alternative Directors" slate, which had pledged to accept the $89 per share offer. 1979

Superior Court upholds PUCA decision that proceeds from land sales inure to customers, not shareholders.

7/3/79 RWA and NHWC agree on seven point merger proposal at $83 per share and proceeds from some land sales.

3/4/80 RWA and NHWC Directors approve final acquisition plan.

8/26/80 The South Central Connecticut Regional Water Authority acquires ownership of New Haven Water Company.

CONTRACT BETWEEN THE CITY OF NEW HAVEN AND THE NEW HAVEN WATER COMPANY

[Contract signed February 17, 1902.]

THIS AGREEMENT, made by and between the City of New Haven and The New Haven Water Company, witnesseth as follows:

First—Said Company will furnish said City with a full and adequate supply of water for all reasonable present and future public and municipal purposes whatsoever, wheresoever the mains of said Company now are or may hereafter be extended within the present limits of the City and within any future limits thereof, including water for school and fire protection purposes, whenever ordered by the City to do so, in the Thirteenth, Fourteenth and Fifteenth wards, for all time after the twentieth day of February, A.D. 1902, or until the termination of this contract in accordance with the provisions thereof, without cost or charge, in consideration of the promises hereinafter set forth.

Second—If said Company shall willfully neglect or refuse to supply said City with water in all respects in conformity with the true intent and meaning of these presents, and a loss by fire shall happen within said City to the property or any person or corporation, in consequence of such neglect or refusal, then said Company shall pay said City ten thousand dollars ($10,000). But said City shall not thereby be precluded from recovering damages actually suffered in its corporate capacity by reason of any breach of this contract.

And if the works of said Company shall at any time prove inadequate for the above named purposes and uses, said City shall have the privilege of annulling this contract, without prejudice to any claims for damages already accrued, or to any right of purchase in accordance with the provisions hereof; provided, however, that in case such inadequacy shall be due to accident, extraordinary drouth, or other cause beyond the control of said Company, said Company shall not be liable to damages or this contract liable to annulment, if said Company shall use all reasonable means to restore said works to a proper state of efficiency; and if this contract shall be so annulled, said Company shall immediately thereafter purchase all the hydrants of said City connected with the mains of said Company, at their actual cost less a reasonable deduction for decay and damage.

Third—Said Company shall notify said City when about to lay down new mains, and shall put in hydrant branches at the expense of said Company, at points designated by authority of the Common Council of said City; and the opening of streets for the laying of mains and location of hydrants, both public and private, in said streets, shall be under the direction of the Director of Public Works, or such other officer of said City as may at any time hereafter be responsible for the care and management of the streets of said City. Said City shall have the right to connect hydrants, at its own expense, with the mains of said Company, at any and all points, at the option of said City, and said hydrants shall be in the exclusive use and under the exclusive control of said City, without hindrance or obstruction in any manner by said Company, but said hydrants shall be used only for the above named purposes and uses; and whatever a hydrant is to be inserted or removed by said City, a reasonable notice shall be given to said Company, and the flow of water shall be shut off by said Company a reasonable time to allow such change to be made. Said City shall have the right, for the above-named uses and purposes, of any hydrant or hydrants which the above named Company may have in use for its own purposes, whenever an engineer of said City Fire Department shall deem it necessary.

Fourth—Said City will from time to time, at the request of said Company (as in course of time the facilities of said Company may be diminished by accident, drouth, or increase of consumption), adopt and enforce reasonable rules and regulations to prevent unreasonable and excessive use and waste of water by its agents and officials. In case of the failure of the City so to do, the Company may adopt such regulations, provided the same be approved by the highest trial court in the State, or a judge thereof, upon application of said Company, after notice to the City and hearing thereon.

Fifth—Said Company agrees that the rates for water, to be

charged to all consumers of water in said City, shall at all times be fair and reasonable; and if said City of New Haven shall at any time consider the rates so charged for water to be unreasonable and the City and the Company cannot agree with reference thereto, the matter shall be submitted to arbitration as hereinafter provided. It is agreed, however, that said arbitrators shall not fix a rate for water which shall leave to said Company an income insufficient to provide means with which to pay its operating costs, including interest on indebtedness, and all labor, material, salaries, damages, renewals, or extensions, repair and replacement of plant, and all taxes, together with a sum sufficient to pay the present rate of dividend upon its present capital stock, and a reasonable return upon such other capital as shall in the future be invested in additions or extensions of the plant of the Company not exceeding the present rate of dividend. Said arbitrators may provide that any class or classes of service shall be paid for by meter and not by fixture rates. Said arbitration, when confirmed by the Court appointing the arbitrators, shall be final and conclusive upon the parties as to the rates to be paid for water, for a period of at least five years from the date of said arbitration report. Said Water Company agrees that whenever, in the opinion of its Directors, its income exceeds the sum required to properly care for the above mentioned purposes, it will, from time to time, as it may be able, without the necessity of arbitration, reduce its rates for water to the inhabitants of the City of New Haven.

The rates to be charged by the City of New Haven Water Company to the consumers of water in the City of New Haven, except as said rates may be changed as above provided, from and after May 1st, 1902, are shown by the following schedule, and said rates shall at all times be as low as therein shown, or lower;

SCHEDULE

ANNUAL WATER RATES OF THE CITY OF NEW HAVEN WATER COMPANY

1. *Sinks, Bowls, and Faucets:*
   For each dwelling occupied by one family, for sink use.....$5.00

This $5 rate shall include any number of ordinary house hold sinks and the use of water for any other household pur poses not otherwise rated below.

Occupied by one family, additional for all set-tubs or set-bowls (either or both). $0.50

Occupied by two families, sink use for each family 4.50

Occupied by two families or more, additional for all set tubs or set-bowls (either or both) for each family. 50

2. *Dwellings Occupied by Two Families or More*, all using same sink, for each family. 4.00

For any greater number of families, or separate occupants, such rates as may be fixed by the Directors.

3. Large Boarding Houses. . . . .$10.00 and upwards.

4. Hotels. 25.00

5. Stores and Warehouses. 5.00

    Offices. 3.00

6. Fish Markets and Saloon sinks. .6.00

7. Photograph Galleries. 10.00

    Meters only for running streams.

8. Barber Shops 6.00

9. *Water Closets and Urinals:*

    Water closets for one family, first closet. 3.00

    Each additional closet for same family 2.00

    Water closet used by more than one family additional 1.00 for each family.

    Boarding houses, first closet. 5.00

    Each additional closet 3.00

    Hotels, first closet 6.00

    Each additional closet 4.00

    Restaurants and Saloons, first close. . . . . . . 5.00 and upwards.

    Each additional 3.00

    Restaurant and Saloon urinals (self-closing), first. . . . . . 4.00 and upwards.

    Each additional 3.00

    Outside closets . . . . 5.00 and upwards.

10. *Bath Tubs:*

    Bath tub for one family 3.00

        Each additional for the same family 2.00

    Boarding Houses, first tub. 5.00

        Each additional 3.00

    Hotels and Public Bath Rooms, first tub. 6.00

        Each additional. . . . . 5.00 and upwards.

11. *Beer Pumps* . . . . 5.00 and upwards.

12. *Bottle Washers* . . . . 3.00 and upwards.

    The above rates do not include the use of hose for any purpose.

13. *Hose (Hand use only):*

    Street use, 30 feet front or less 3.00

    Each additional lineal foot. 08

    Lawns and gardens, frontage 30 feet or less 2.00

     "   "   "   30 to 50 feet. 3.00

     "   "   "   50 to 60 feet. 4.00

     "   "   "   60 to 75 feet 5.00

     "   "   "   75 to 100 feet 6.00

    For each additional hose fixture for the same frontage . . 1.00

Revolving Sprinklers of any kind, movable fixtures or hose used in
any other way then by hand, for use of four hours or less per
day. 10.00

    Flowing fountains on measured service only.

14. *Stables:*

    Private stables, including carriage washing, one horse . . 3.00

        Each additional horse. 2.00

    Livery Stables, each horse 2.00

    Cow Stables, each cow. 1.00

15. *Bakeries:*

    For the daily average use of flour, in addition to fixtures
rates,   per barrel 3.00

16. *Steam Use:*

    Stationary Engine, from 1 to 10 h.p., each h.p. 6.00

"	"	from 10 to 50 h.p., each h.p 5.00
"	"	from 50 to 100 h.p., each h.p 4.00
"	"	above 100 h.p 3.00

17. Building Purposes:

Brick, per thousand (plain) 0.05

Brick, per thousand (including plastering 10

Plastering, per 100 yards $0.30

Stone Work, each barrel of lime 06

Stone Work, each barrel of cement. 03

18. *In all cases* where water is required for purposes not specified above, the rates shall be fixed by the Board of Directors.

METER RATES

	cu.ft.	gal.
1. 134 cubic ft. (1,00 gallons) or less per day, per 100	13 1/2c	.018c
134 cubic ft. to 400 cubic ft. (1,000 to 3,000 gallons) per day, per 100	10 1/2c	.014c
400 cubic ft. (3,000 gallons) and over per day, per 100	07 1/2c	.01c

All metered water will be charged for, whether used or wasted, and a minimum charge per quarter of $2 will be made on all metered services where the consumption of water is less than the above.

If a meter gets out of order and fails to register, the consumer will be charged at the average daily consumption as shown by the meter when in order.

All meters are set by the Water Company, and a proper charge may be made for the work. All damage to the meter will be charged to the owner or occupant of the premises, and in addition to the service-rate a yearly rental of one dollar for each five-eighths will be collected, larger sizes in proportion.

Any consumer may, subject to the regulations of the Company, be put upon a metered service, if he shall so desire.

And said Company agrees that if ever it shall violate any of its promises or stipulations in this article contained, said City, or any person injured by such violation, shall be entitled to recover from said Company the damages sustained by such person by such violation;

and in case of judgment in favor of the plaintiff in any suit brought in such case in the name of said City, the damages shall be fixed at not less than twenty dollars.

Sixth—Said Company agrees to use all reasonable efforts to supply said City and its inhabitants with pure and wholesome water. It being understood that plans for the filtration of the Lake Whitney supply are now under consideration by the Company,

Seventh—Said Company shall not refuse to supply water to any person who shall be ready and willing to pay the established rated therefor, if there shall be a water main in the street adjacent to the property owned or occupied by such person or persons, or if such persons shall be ready and willing to lay from any main a suitable pipe or pipes for that purpose; and in case of such refusal, every person who may be injured thereby shall be entitled to recover just damages therefor, which damages shall be fixed at not less than twenty dollars.

Eighth—If at any time it shall be finally determined in or by judicial proceedings that said Company has not complied with the terms hereof, either with respect to the supply or the quality of the water furnished to said City and its inhabitants, or if at any time said Company shall have refused to abide by the result of the arbitration or arbitrations on the matters hereinbefore provided to be arbitrated between them, then said City shall thereupon have the right to purchase all the property, assets and franchises of said Company, upon paying to it a just and fair compensation therefor, which compensation, if said parties cannot agree, shall be determined by a committee to be appointed by the Superior Court in the manner provided by the Act passed by the General Assembly at its January session, 1881, or, if said Superior Court does not then exists, by the highest trial court then in existence in the State; but the City shall commence to take steps for such judicial purchase within four months from such judicial determination or refusal.

Ninth—Whenever it shall be claimed by said City that cause exists for the annulment of this contract by reason of any breach thereof, and said City shall desire that said contract be annulled, it may, through its proper officers, provide its application to the highest court of original jurisdiction, alleging such breach, and praying that said contract be annulled by reason thereof. Wherever arbitration is provided for in this contract, except the Eighth Article hereof, said arbitration shall be made by a committee composed of three persons to be appointed by such court.

Tenth—Said Company shall pay such taxes as may be levied according to law upon its tangible property, including pipes, mains and reservoirs, within the City of New Haven and other towns in which such property may be located. In case any franchise or other tax, except upon its tangible property, shall be assessed against said Company, said City shall save said Company harmless from such part thereof as shall be measured by the ratio of the gross revenue received from consumers within the City of New Haven, to the gross revenue of said Company from all its consumers. Said City may, at its option, refuse to save said Company harmless, as heretofore provided, and in case of its failure so to do, it shall, without other liability to said Company by reason thereof, pay, during such period of failure, for water for fire protection the sum of twenty dollars per year for each hydrant, and for all other water used by said City at the lowest meter rates to private consumers, as per schedule then in force, less a discount of twenty-five per cent (25%) therefrom.

Eleventh—At the end of twenty-five years from the 20th day of February, A.D. 1902, and at the end of every successive period of twenty-five years thereafter, if said City shall determine to purchase the property, assets and franchises of said Company, said Company will then sell and convey the same to said City upon said City paying a just and fair compensation therefor, which said compensation, if said parties cannot agree, shall be determined by a committee to be appointed by the Superior Court, in the manner provided by the Act passed by the General Assembly at its January session, 1881.

Twelfth—In the case said Company shall sell or transfer its property and franchises to any other person or corporation, or in case the Board of Directors of said Company shall at any time be so constituted that a majority of its members shall not be residents of said City, or in case said Company shall become a member of any trust or syndicate, the said City shall thereupon have the right to purchase the property, assets, and franchises of said Company in the manner set out in Article Eighth hereof.

Thirteenth—Said City agrees to take and use the water so to be furnished by said Company harmless from taxation, as provided in Article Tenth, to pay for said water according to the provisions of Said Article Tenth.

Fourteenth—Neither of the parties hereto shall be at liberty to avoid or set aside this contract, without the consent of the other, notwithstanding any breach thereof, except in the manner provided herein.

Fifteenth—Said City and said Company will unite in an application to the General Assembly, at its next session, for the passage of an act making the terms of this contract obligatory upon both parties as though specifically authorized in their respective charters.

IN WITNESS WHEREOF, said parties have severally caused their respective corporate names to be signed, and their respective corporate seals to be affixed to this instrument, and to a duplicate and triplicate instrument of the same tenor and date, this 17th day of February, A.D. 1902; said City acting herein by its Mayor, the Honorable John P. Studley, hereunto duly authorized; and said Company acting herein by its committee, Eli Whitney, James English, and George D. Watrous, who are hereunto duly authorized and empowered by a vote of the Directors of said Company.

THE CITY OF NEW HAVEN,

[CITY SEAL.]   By John P. Studley, *Mayor.*

THE NEW HAVEN WATER COMPANY,

[COMPANY SEAL.]   By Eli Whitney
                                   James English
                                   George D. Watrous

Its Committee hereunto duly authorized.

Contract approved as to form.
    Leonard M. Daggett
    Corporation Counsel.

ADDITIONAL STIPULATION TO CITY CONTRACT.

THE NEW HAVEN WATER COMPANY hereby stipulates that, at the option of the City of New Haven, the contract this day entered into between said Company and said City may be so construed that nothing therein contained shall prevent said City from sinking or driving wells in its parks, squares, and other public property, and pumping water therefrom to be used upon the premises where pumped and such part of the highway as is immediately adjacent thereto; provided, however, that water shall not be distributed by the City either for public or private purposes, in pipes or mains.

And further so construed that in no case shall any person be charged any higher price for a continuance of his present service, that he has heretofore been charged for the same service, unless changed by arbitration as provided in said contract.

It is further stipulated that stipulated shall, at the option of said City, be made to the General Assembly for the confirmation hereof, at the same time when said contract is presented for confirmation.

Dated at New Haven, this 17th day of February, 1902.

THE NEW HAVEN WATER COMPANY,
By Eli Whitney
[L.S.]   J. English
George D. Watrous
Its Committee hereunto duly authorized.

REPORT OF THE COMMITTEE ON WATER DE EXTENSION OF SERVICE TO THE 13TH, 14TH, AND 15TH WARDS.

To the Honorable Court of Common Council of the City of New Haven:

Your Committee on Water to whom has referred the Resolution de Water Supply for school and fire purposes in the Thirteenth, Fourteenth and Fifteenth Wards, beg leave to report that they have attended to the business assigned, and on due examination are of the option that the prayer of said petitioner should be granted.

They therefore respectfully recommend the passage of the following order.

All of which is respectfully submitted,

EDWARD FERTMAN, *Chairman.*

Ordered that the New Haven Water Company be and is hereby ordered and required to furnish a full an adequate supply of water for fire protection and school purposes in the Thirteenth, Fourteenth and Fifteenth Wards, in accordance with the provisions of Paragraph First of the Contract, recently entered into between the City of New Haven and the New Haven Water Company.

Board of Alderman, April 7, 1902.
Read, accepted and order passed.

HENRY E. NORRIS, *City Clerk.*

Board of Councilmen, April 14, 1902.
Concurred.

JAMES B. MARTIN, *Assistant City Clerk.*

City of New Haven, April 23, 1902.
Approved,

JOHN P. STUDLEY, *Mayor.*

PUBLIC ACT NO. 77-606

AN ACT CONCERNING THE COUNCIL ON WATER COMPANY LANDS.

Section 1. (NEW) The general assembly finds and declares that an adequate supply of pure water is and will always be essential for the health and safety and economic well-being of the state, that lands acquired for public water supply purposes are and will in the future be necessary to protect the public water supply notwithstanding the availability of water filtration plants; that some of such lands have been acquired by water companies having the power of eminent domain, that such lands are in imminent danger of being disposed of by water companies for residential and commercial development, that such lands constitute a significant portion of the remaining undeveloped and open space lands in close proximity to the urbanized areas of the state, and that it is in the public interest that there be established criteria for the orderly disposition of such lands. The general assembly further finds and declares that in order to protect the purity and adequacy of the water supply the department of health should be directed to revise its procedure for the review of applications to sell water company land located on public drinking water supply watersheds, that the disposition of such land prior to the revision of application review procedures would jeopardize the public health and welfare, and that therefore the prohibition against sale or development of water company land located on the watershed should be extended for a period of two years from the effective date of this act.

Sec. 2. (NEW) As used in this act, "critical components of a stream belt" means (1) the water course of a defined stream including banks, beds and water: (2) land subject to stream overflow: (3) associated wetlands, and (4) shorelines of lakes and ponds associated with the stream. "First-order stream" means a stream which directly enters a reservoir: "purity and adequacy of public drinking water supply" means the quality and quantity of public drinking water as determined by the public health council under subsection (d) of section 25-32 of the general statutes, and "commissioner" means the commissioner of health.

Sec. 3. (NEW) The department of health shall adopt, in accordance with chapter 54 of the general statutes, regulations establishing criteria and performance standards for three classes of water company owned land.

(a) Class I land includes all land owned by a water company which is either: (1) Within two hundred and fifty feet of high water of a reservoir or one hundred feet of all watercourses as defined in agency regulations adopted pursuant to section 19-13 of the general statutes; (2) within the areas along watercourses which are covered by any of the critical components of a stream belt; (3) land with slopes fifteen per cent or greater without significant interception by wetlands, swales and natural depressions between the slopes and the water courses; (4) within two hundred feet of groundwater wells; (5) an identified direct recharge area or outcrop of aquifer now in use or available for future use, or (6) an area with shallow depth to bedrock, twenty inches or less, or poorly drained or very poorly drained soils as defined by the United States Soil Conservation Service that are contiguous to land described in subdivisions (3) or (4) of this subsection and that extend to the top of the slope above the receiving watercourse.

(b) Class II land includes all land owned by a water company which is either (1) on a public drinking supply watershed which is not included in Class I or (2) completely off a public drinking supply watershed and which is within one hundred and fifty feet of a distribution reservoir or a first-order stream tributary to a distribution reservoir.

(c) Class III land includes all land owned by a water company which is unimproved land off public drinking supply watersheds and beyond one hundred and fifty feet from a distribution reservoir or first-order stream tributary to a distribution reservoir.

Sec. 4. Section 25-32 of the general statutes is repealed and the following is substituted in lieu thereof:

(a) The state department of health shall have jurisdiction over all matters concerning the purity and adequacy of any source of water or ice supply used by any municipality, public institution or water or ice company for obtaining water or ice, the safety of any distributing plant and system for public health purposes, the adequacy of methods used to assure water purity, and such other matters relating to the construction and operation of such distributing plant and system as may affect public health. The qualifications of the operators of plants for the treatment of water furnished or intended to be furnished to any such water supply shall be subject to the approval of said department.

(b) No water company shall sell, lease, ASSIGN or otherwise dispose of or change the use of any watershed lands, except as provided in section 25-43c without [the prior approval of] A WRITTEN PERMIT FROM the state commissioner of health. [Any water company which proposes such disposition or change in the usage of such land shall submit to the commissioner of health a statement analyzing the effect of such proposed disposition or change on the purity and adequacy of the water supply and on maintenance of ground water supplies under the most severe climatic conditions. Within sixty days after receipt of such change of usage proposal, said commissioner shall issue a decision to said water company approving or disapproving such proposal and setting forth his reasons for such approval or disapproval, and shall forward a copy of such decision to the state public utilities control authority. The state public health council shall, in its public health code, adopt standards for the approval or disapproval of such proposed disposition or change in the usage of such watershed land.] SAID COMMISSIONER SHALL NOT GRANT A PERMIT FOR THE SALE, LEASE OR ASSIGNMENT OF CLASS I LAND, AND SHALL NOT GRANT A PERMIT FOR A CHANGE IN USE OF CLASS I LAND UNLESS THE APPLICANT DEMONSTRATES THAT SUCH CHANGE WILL NOT HAVE HAVE A SIGNIFICANT ADVERSE IMPACT UPON THE PRESENT AND FUTURE PURITY AND ADEQUACY OF THE PUBLIC DRINKING WATER SUPPLY.

(c) THE COMMISSIONER OF HEALTH MAY GRANT A PERMIT FOR THE SALE, LEASE, ASSIGNMENT OR CHANGE IN USE OF ANY LAND IN CLASS II SUBJECT TO ANY CONDITIONS OR RESTRICTION IN USE WHICH THE COMMISSIONER MAY DEEM NECESSARY TO MAINTAIN THE PURITY AND

ADEQUACY OF THE PUBLIC DRINKING WATER SUPPLY, GIVING DUE CONSIDERATION TO (1) THE CREATION OF POINT OR NON-POINT SOURCES OF CONTAMINATION; (2) THE DISTURBANCE OF GROUND VEGETATION; (3) THE CREATION OF SUBSURFACE SEWAGE DISPOSAL SYSTEMS; (4) THE DEGREE OF WATER TREATMENT PROVIDED, AND (5) ANY OTHER SIGNIFICANT POTENTIAL SOURCE OF CONTAMINATION OF THE PUBLIC DRINKING WATER SUPPLY.

(d) THE COMMISSIONER SHALL NOT GRANT A PERMIT FOR THE SALE, LEASE, ASSIGNMENT OR CHANGE IN USE OF ANY LAND IN CLASS II UNLESS THE APPLICANT DEMONSTRATES THAT THE PROPOSED SALE, LEASE, ASSIGNMENT OR CHANGE IN USE WILL NOT HAVE A SIGNIFICANT ADVERSE IMPACT UPON THE PURITY AND ADEQUACY OF THE PUBLIC DRINKING WATER SUPPLY AND THAT ANY USE RESTRICTIONS WHICH THE COMMISSIONER REQUIRES AS A CONDITION OF GRANTING A PERMIT CAN BE ENFORCED AGAINST SUBSEQUENT OWNERS, LESSEES AND ASSIGNEES.

[(c)] (e) The term "source of water or ice supply" includes all springs, streams, watercourses, brooks, rivers, ponds, wells or underground waters from which water or ice is taken, and all springs, streams, watercourses, brooks, rivers, lakes, ponds, wells or underground waters tributary thereto and all lands drained thereby; and the term "watershed land" means land from which water drains into a public drinking water supply.

[(d)] (f) The public health council shall adopt and from time to time may amend the following: (1) Physical, chemical, radiological and microbiological standards for the quality of public drinking water; (2) minimum treatment methods, taking into account the costs thereof, required for all sources of drinking water, including guidelines for the design and operation of treatment works and water sources, which guidelines shall serve as the basis for approval of local water supply plans by the commissioner of health, AND (3) MINIMUM STANDARDS TO ASSURE THE LONG-TERM PURITY AND ADEQUACY OF THE PUBLIC DRINKING WATER SUPPLY TO ALL RESIDENTS OF THIS STATE. On or after October 1,

1975, any water company which requests approval of any drinking water source shall provide for such treatment methods as specified by the public health council, provided any water company in operation prior to October 1, 1975, and having such source shall comply with regulations adopted by the public health council in conformance with The Safe Drinking Water Act, Public Law 93-523, and shall submit on or before February 1, 1976, a statement of intent to provide for treatment methods as specified by said council, to the commissioner of health for the approval.

[(e)] (g) The department of health may perform the collection and testing of water samples required by regulations adopted pursuant to this section when requested to do so by the water company. The department shall collect a fee equal to the cost of such collection and testing. Water companies serving one thousand or more persons shall not request routine bacteriological or physical tests.

Sec. 5. (NEW) Within two years after the effective date of this act, the commissioner shall adopt regulations in accordance with chapter 54 of the general statutes for the review of permit applications. Such procedure shall include a standard application form, a public hearing and enforcement provisions. If, in the judgment of the commissioner, the proposed sale, lease, assignment or change in use of Class II land may have a significant adverse impact upon the applicant's water supply, said commissioner shall, within thirty days of his receipt of a complete permit application, refer such application to a professional review team appointed by said commissioner, consisting of a professional water supply engineer from the staff of the public utilities control authority; a professional from the staff of the department of environmental protection with expertise in one of the following areas: Water supply, hydrology, aquatic biology, forestry, geology or other related fields; a professionals planner recommended by the chief executive officer of the town or towns in which the land proposed for disposition is located; a professional planner from the staff of the department of health and up to three other experts in the public health field. No appointee shall serve at the time of his appointment in the employ of the applicant. Such team shall evaluate the impact of the proposed sale, lease, assignment or change in use if land upon the purity and adequacy of the water supply infer the most severe climatic conditions and its ability to meet current water standards adopted by the department of health.

Sec. 6. (NEW) Within sixty days after the receipt of a complete permit application the commissioner of health shall issue a written decision granting or denying the permit and setting forth the reasons for his decision, provided, if the commissioner has utilized the services of a professional review team as provided for by section 5 of this act, such review team shall submit to said commissioner, within ninety days of his receipt of such application, a written report of its findings, and said commissioner shall issue decision within one hundred and twenty days of his decision to the applicant, the public utilities control authority, the department of environmental protection and the chief executive officer of the town in which the land is located.

Sec. 7. (NEW) The commissioner of health shall submit a report to the general assembly on or before December 1, 1980, evaluating the application and review procedures and the land classification system establishment pursuant to this act and recommended such amendments to this act as said commissioner deems necessary to better effectuate the purposes of this act.

Sec. 8. (NEW) No water company land classified under section 3 of this act as Class II land shall be sold, leased or assigned for a period of two years from the effective date of this act, or until the final adoption of regulations by the commissioner of health as required in section 5 of this act, whichever occurs first.

Sec. 9. The sum of five thousand dollars is appropriated to the department of health for the fiscal year ending June 30, 1978, from the sum appropriated to the finance advisory committee under section 1 of substitute house bill 7854 of the current session, for 1977 acts without appropriations, to carry out the purposes of this act.

Sec. 10. This act shall take effect from its passage.
Approved June 26, 1977.

Appendix E

Substitute House Bill No. 7958

SPECIAL ACT NO. 77-98

AN ACT CONCERNING FINANCIAL ASSISTANCE FOR WATER COMPANIES FOR CONSTRUCTION OF TREATMENT FACILITIES AND CREATING THE SOUTH CENTRAL CONNECTICUT REGIONAL WATER AUTHORITY.

Section 1. It is found and declared as a matter of legislative determination that the creation of the South Central Connecticut Regional Water Authority for the primary purpose of providing and assuring the provision of an adequate supply of pure water at reasonable cost within the South Central Connecticut Regional Water District and, to the degree consistent with the foregoing, of advancing the conservation and compatible recreational use of land held by the authority, and the carrying out of its powers, purposes, and duties under sections 1 to 33, inclusive, of this act are for the benefit of the people in the South Central Connecticut Regional Water District and the State of Connecticut, and for the improvement of their health, safety, welfare, that said purposes are public purposes, and that the authority will be performing an essential governmental function in the exercise of its powers under sections 1 to 33, inclusive, of this act.

Sec. 2. As used in sections 1 to 33, inclusive, of this act, unless a different meaning appears, in the context: "Authority" means the South Central Connecticut Regional Water Authority created by section 5 of this act: "district" means the South Central Connecticut Regional Water District created by section 3 of this act; "representative policy board" means the representative policy board of the South Central Connecticut Regional Water District created by section 4 of this act: "chief executive officer" means that full time employee of the authority responsible for the execution of the policies of the authority and for the direction of the other employees of the authority: "treasurer" means the treasurer of the authority: "customer" means any person, firm, corporation, company, association or governmental unit furnished water service by the authority or any owner of property who guarantees payment for water service to such property; "properties" means the water supply and distribution system or systems and other real or personal property of the authority; "bonds" means bonds, notes and other obligations issued by the authority; "revenues" means all rents, charges and other income derived from the operation of the properties of the authority; "water supply system" means plants, structures and other real and personal property acquired, constructed or operated for the purpose of supplying water, including land, reservoirs, basins, dams, canals, aqueducts, standpipes, conduits, pipelines, mains, pumping stations, water distribution systems, compensating reservoirs, waterworks or sources of water supply, wells, purification or filtration plants or other plants and works, connections, rights of flowage or diversion and other plants, structures, conveyances, real or personal property or rights therein and appurtenances necessary or useful and convenient for the accumulation, supply or distribution of water. A reference in sections 1 to 33, inclusive, of this act, to any general statute, public act or special act shall include any amendment or successor thereto.

Sec. 3. There is created a district to be known as the "South Central Connecticut Water District" which embraces the area and territory of the towns and cities of Bethany, Branford, Cheshire, East Haven, Guilford, Hamden, Killingworth, Madison, Milford, New Haven, North Branford, North Haven, Orange, Prospect, Wallingford, West Haven and Woodbridge; provided, in the event the authority shall at any time in the future acquire land or properties or sell water directly to customers in other cities or towns within the state, the district shall be enlarged to embrace the area and territory of such cities or towns; and provided further, in the event at any time after five years after the effective date of this act, the authority shall neither own land or properties nor sell water directly to customers in any city or town within the district, the area and territory of such city or town thereupon shall be excluded from the district.

Sec. 4. (a) There shall be a representative policy board of the

South Central Connecticut Regional Water District which shall consist of one elector from each city and town within the district who shall be appointed by the chief elected official of such city or town, with the approval of its legislative body. Members shall serve for a term of three years commencing July 1, except that the members first appointed shall serve terms commencing July 1, 1977, and such members appointed from Bethany, East Haven, Killingworth, New Haven, Orange and West Haven shall serve until June 30, 1978, such members appointed from Branford, Guilford, Madison, North Branford, Prospect and Woodbridge shall serve until June 30, 1979, such members appointed from Cheshire, Hamden, Milford, North Haven and Wallingford shall serve until June 30, 1980, and members first appointed from cities or towns added to the district as provided in section 3 of this act shall serve terms commencing upon appointment and ending on the third June thirtieth thereafter; provided members shall continue to serve until their successors are appointed and have qualified. In the event of the resignation, death or disability of a member from any city or town, a successor may be appointed by the chief elected official of such city or town for the unexpired portion of the term. The chief elected official of each such city or town may appoint a provisional member to serve until December 1, 1977, with full authority to act as a member until said date. Members and provisional members shall receive fifty dollars for each day in which they are engaged in their duties and shall be reimbursed for their necessary expenses incurred in the performance of their duties. They shall elect a chairman and a vice-chairman, who shall be members or provisional members of the representative policy board, and a secretary. The representative policy board shall meet at least quarterly with the authority and such members of the staff of the authority as the representative policy board deems appropriate.

(b) In voting upon all matters before the representative policy board, the vote of each member shall be accorded a weight, determined as follows: The sum of (1) the quotient obtained by dividing the number of customers in the city or town from which such member is appointed by the total number of customers in all cities and towns from which members have been appointed, taken twice, and (2) the quotient obtained by dividing the number of acres of land owned by the authority within the city or town from which such member is appointed by the total number of acres of land owned by the authority in all cities and towns from which members have been appointed, shall be divided by three, the quotient thereof multiplied by one hundred and the product thereof shall be rounded to the nearest whole number. For the purposes of this section, "number of customers" means the number of premises or groups of premises treated as units for ordinary billing or other ordinary receipt of charges by the authority and shall be determined from the records of the authority on the last day of its preceding fiscal year and "number of acres of land" means the number of acres of land rounded to the nearest whole number as may appear on the records of the authority on the last day of its preceding fiscal year. Notwithstanding the foregoing, prior to the first day of the fiscal year of the authority commencing after the acquisition by the authority of a water supply system, the weighed vote of each member of the representative policy board shall be as follows: Bethany, four, Branford, seven; Cheshire, three; East Haven, six; Guilford, four; Hamden, twelve; Killingworth, one; Madison, six; Milford, eleven; New Haven, seventeen; North Branford, eight; North Haven, four; Orange, three; Prospect, one; Wallingford, one; West Haven, ten; and Woodbridge, two. Whenever a vote is taken on any matter by the representative policy board, the vote shall be determined in accordance with this subsection. Members of the representative policy board holding a majority of the votes so weighted shall constitute a quorum.

(c) The representative policy board shall adopt and may amend such rules of procedure and bylaws for the conduct of its affairs as it deems appropriate. It shall establish (1) a standing committee on land use and management to consult with the authority on all matters of land use and management, including acquisition and sale, recreational use, cutting of timber and other products, mining and quarrying; (2) a standing committee on finance to consult with the authority on matters relating to financial and budgetary matters and the establishment of rates; and (3) a standing committee on consumer affairs to consult with the authority and the office of consumer affairs established pursuant to section 15 of this act on matters concerning the interests of people residing within the district. The representative policy board may appoint such other committees as it considers from time to time.

Sec. 5. A public corporation, to be known as the "South Central Connecticut Regional Water Authority," is created for the purposes, charges with the duties and granted the powers provided in sections 1 to 33, inclusive, of this act. The authority shall consist of five members who shall not be members of the representative policy board, who shall be residents of the district and who shall be appointed without regard to political affiliation by a majority of the total votes of those members of the representative policy board present at a meeting at which members of said board holding two-thirds of the total votes are present, for terms of five years and until their successors are appointed and have qualified, except that of the members first appointed, one shall be appointed for a term ending January 1, 1983, one for a term ending January 1, 1982, one for a term ending January 1, 1981, one for a term ending January 1, 1980, and one for a term ending January 1, 1979. Any vacancy occurring on the authority shall be filled in the same manner for the unexpired portion of the term. Any member of the authority may be removed from office by the representative policy board for cause. Members of the authority shall receive such compensation for their services as shall be fixed by the representative policy board and shall be reimbursed for their necessary expenses incurred in performance of their duties.

Sec. 6. The duration of the representative policy board and of the authority shall be perpetual unless terminated or altered by act of the general assembly, provided the general assembly shall not terminate the existence of the authority until all of its liabilities have been met and its bonds have been paid in full or such liabilities and bonds have otherwise been discharged.

Sec. 7. The officers of the authority shall be a chairman and a vice chairman, who shall be members of the authority, and a treasurer and a secretary, who may be members of the authority. The first chairman shall be designated by the representative policy board for a two-year term and subsequent chairmen shall be elected by the authority for two year terms. All other officers shall be elected by the authority for one year terms. The treasurer shall execute a bond, conditioned upon the faithful performance of the duties of his office, the amount and sufficiency of which shall be approved by the authority and the premium therefore shall be paid by the authority. The authority shall, from time to time, appoint an agent for the service of process, and shall notify the secretary of the state of name and address of said agent.

Sec. 8. The authority may employ such persons as it may determine to be necessary or convenient for the performance of its duties and may fix and determine their qualifications, duties and compensations, provided the appointment of the chief executive officer shall be subject to the approval of the representative policy board. The authority shall establish a position with ongoing responsibilities for the use and management of its land resources and such other senior managerial positions as it deems appropriate, which shall be filled by appointment by the chief executive officer with the approval of the authority. The authority may also from time to time contract for professional services.

Sec. 9. The authority shall meet at least monthly. Except as the bylaws of the authority may provide in emergency situations, the powers of the authority shall be exercised by the members at a meeting duly called and held. Three members shall constitute a quorum, and no action shall be taken except pursuant to the affirmative vote of at least three members. The authority may delegate to one or more of its members, officers, agents or employees such powers and duties as it may deem proper.

Sec. 10. Whenever a public hearing is required under sections 1 to 33, inclusive, of this act, notice of such hearing shall be published by the representative policy board at least twenty days before the date set therefor, in the newspaper or newspapers having a general circulation in each city and town comprising the district. Such notice shall set forth the date, time and place of such hearing and shall include a description of the matters to be considered at such hearing. A copy of the notice shall be filed in the office of the clerk of each city and town and shall be available for inspection by the public. At such hearings, all the users of the water supply system, owners of property served or to be served and other interested persons shall have an opportunity to be heard concerning the matters under consideration. When appropriate, the chairman of the representative policy board may convene more than one hearing on any matter and direct such hearings to be held in suitable locations within the district so as to assure broader participation by the general public in discussion of the matters under consideration, provided in the case of the sale or transfer of real property pursuant to section 18 of this act a public hearing shall be held in the city or town in which such real property is situated. Any decision of the representative policy board on matters considered at such public hearing shall be in writing and shall be published in a newspaper or newspapers having a general circulation in each city and town comprising the district within thirty days after such decision is made.

Sec. 11. Subject to the provisions of sections 1 to 33, inclusive, of this act, the authority shall have the power: (a) To sue and be sued; (b) to have a seal and alter the name at its pleasure; (c) to acquire in the name of the authority by purchase, lease or otherwise and to hold and dispose of personal property or any interest therein; (d) to acquire in the name of the authority by purchase, lease or otherwise and to hold and dispose of any real property or interest therein, including water rights and rights of way, which the authority determines to be necessary or convenient, including any existing water supply system or parts thereof, situated wholly or partially within the district. As a means of so acquiring, the authority may purchase all of the stock or all or any part of the assets and franchises of any existing privately owned water company, whereupon the authority shall succeed to all rights, powers and franchises thereof. Sections 16-43, 16-50c and 16-50d of the general statutes shall not apply to any action by the authority or any action by any privately owned water company, as defined in section 16-1 of the general statutes, taken to effectuate the acquisition of the stock or all or any part of the assets and franchises of such water company by the authority; (e) to construct and develop any water supply system; (f) to own, operate, maintain, repair, improve, construct, reconstruct, replace, enlarge and extend any of its properties; (g) any provision in any general statute, special act or charter to the contrary notwithstanding, but subject to the provisions of sections 12 and 28 of this act, to sell water, however acquired, to customers within the district or to any municipality or water company; (h) any provisions in any general statute, special act or charter to the contrary notwithstanding, to purchase water approved by the commissioner of health from any person, private corporation or municipality when necessary or convenient for the operation of any water supply system operated by the authority; (i) to adopt and amend bylaws, rules and regulations for the management and regulation of its affairs and for the use of its properties and, subject to the provisions of any resolution authorizing the issuance of bonds, rules for the sale of water and the collection of rents and charges therefor. A copy of such by laws, rules and regulations and all amendments thereto, certified by the secretary of the authority, shall be filed in the office of the secretary of the state and with the clerk of each town and city within the district; (j) to make contracts and to execute all necessary or convenient instruments, including evidences of indebtedness, negotiable or non-negotiable; (k) to borrow money, to issue negotiable bonds or notes, to fund and refund the same and to provide for the rights of the holders of the authority's obligations; (l) to open the grounds in any public street or way or public for the purpose of laying, installing, maintaining or replacing pipes and conduits, provided upon the completion of such work the grounds shall be restored to the condition they were previously; (m) to enter into cooperative agreements with other water authorities, municipalities, water districts or water companies within or without the district for interconnection of facilities, for exchange or interchange of services and commodities or for any other lawful purpose necessary or desirable to effect the purposes of sections 1 to 33, inclusive, of this act, such agreements to be binding for a period specified therein; (n) to acquire, hold, develop and maintain land and other real estate and waters for conservation and for compatible active and passive recreational purposes and to levy charges for such uses, provided the state department of health finds that such uses will not harm the quality of water provided by the authority; (o) to apply for and accept grants, loans or contributions from the United States, the state of Connecticut or any agency, instrumentality or subdivision of wether of them or from any person, and to expend the proceeds for any of its purposes; (p) to do any and all things necessary or convenient to carry out the powers expressly given in sections 1 to 33, inclusive, of this act, including the powers granted by the general statutes to stock corporations, except the power to issue stock.

Sec. 12. The authority shall not sell water to customers in any part of the district with respect to which any person, any firm or any corporation incorporated under the general statutes or any special act has been granted a franchise to operate as a water company, as defined in section 16-1 of the general statutes, or in which any town, city or borough or any district organized for municipal purposes operates a municipal water supply system, unless the legislative body of such town, city, borough or district, such person, or the governing board of such firm or corporation shall consent in writing to such sale by the authority.

Sec. 13. (a) Except with respect to any real or personal property or interest therein, the legal title to which is vested in the state or a political subdivision thereof, or with respect to any existing water supply system, if such authority cannot agree with any owner upon the terms of acquisition by the authority of any real or personal property or interest therein which the authority is authorized to acquire, the authority may proceed, at its election, in the manner provided in subsection (b) or in the manner provided in subsection (c) of this section.

(b) The authority may, after ten days' written notice to such owner, petition the superior court for the county of judicial district in which such property is located, or, if said court is not sitting, any judge of said court, and thereupon said court or such judge shall appoint a committee of three disinterested persons, who shall be sworn before commencing their duties. Such committee, after giving reasonable notice to the parties, shall view the property in questions, hear the evidence, ascertain the value, assess just damages to the owner or parties interested in the property and report its doings to said court or such judge. Within fourteen days after such report is made to said court or such judge, any party may move for the acceptance thereof. Said court or such judge may accept such report or may reject it for irregular or improper conduct by the committee in the performance of its duties. If the report is rejected, the court or judge shall appoint another committee, which shall proceed in the same manner as did the first committee. If the report is accepted, such acceptance shall have the effect of a judgment in favor of the owner of the property against said authority for the amount of such assessment, and, except as otherwise provided by law, execution may issue therefore. Such property shall not be used by such authority until the amount of such assessment has been paid to the party to whom it is due or deposited for his use with the state treasurer and, upon such payment or deposit, such property shall become the property of the authority; provided, if at any stage of condemnation proceedings brought hereunder, it appears to the court or judge before whom such proceedings are pending that the public interest will be prejudiced by delay, said court or such judge may direct that the authority be permitted to enter immediately upon the property to be taken and devote it temporarily to the public use specified in such petition upon the deposit with said court of a sum to be fixed by said court or such judge, upon notice to the parties of not less than ten days, and such sum when so fixed and paid shall be applied so far as it may be necessary for the purpose of the payment of any award of damages which may be made, with interest thereon from the date of the order of said court or judge, and the remainder if any returned to the authority. If such petition is dismissed or no award of damages is made, said court or such judge shall direct that the money so deposited, so far as it may be necessary, shall be applied to the payment of any damages that the owner of such property or other parties in interest may have sustained by such entry upon and use of such property, and of the costs and expenses of such proceedings, such damages to be ascertained by said court or such judge or a committee to be appointed for that purpose, and if the sum so deposited is insufficient to pay such damages and all costs and expenses so awarded, judgment shall be entered against the authority for the deficiency, to be enforced and collected in the same manner as a judgment in the superior court; and the possession of such property shall be restored to the owner or owners thereof. The expenses or costs of any such proceedings shall be taxed by said court or such judge and paid by the authority.

(c) The authority, in its name, may proceed in the manner specified for redevelopment agencies in accordance with sections 8-128 to 8-133, inclusive, of the general statutes.

Sec. 14. With the approval of the representative policy board, the authority shall establish just and equitable rates or charges for the use of the water supply system authorized herein, to be paid by any customer, and may change such rates or charges from time to time. Such rates or charges shall be established so as to provide funds sufficient in each year, with other revenues, if any, (a) to pay the cost of maintaining, repairing and operating the water supply system and each and every portion thereof, to the extent that adequate provision for the payment of such cost has not otherwise been made, (b) to pay the principal of and the interest on outstanding bonds of the authority as the same shall become due and payable, (c) to meet any requirements of any resolution authorizing, or trust agreement securing, such bonds of the authority, (d) to make payments in lieu of taxes as provided in section 21 of this act, as the same become due and payable, upon the properties of the authority to the municipalities in which such properties are situated, (e) to provide for the maintenance, conservation and appropriate recreational use of the land of authority and (f) to pay all other reasonable and necessary expenses of the authority and of the representative policy board. No such rate or charge shall be established until it has been approved by the representative policy board, after said board has held a public hearing at which all the users of the waterworks system, the owners of property served or to be served and other interested have had an opportunity to be heard concerning such proposed rate or charge. The representative policy board shall approve such rates and charges unless it finds that such rates and charges will provide funds in excess of the amounts required for the purposed described previously in this section, or unless it finds that such rates and charges will provide funds insufficient for such purposes. The rates or charges so established for any class of users or property served shall be extended to cover any additional premises thereafter served which are within the same class, without the necessity of a hearing thereon. Any change in such rates or charges shall be made in the same manner in which they were established. Such rates or charges, if not paid when due, shall constitute a lien upon the premises served and a charge against the owners thereof, which lien and charge shall bear interest at the same rate as would unpaid taxes. Such lien shall take precedence over all other liens or encumbrances except taxes and may be foreclosed against the lot or building served in the same manner as alien for taxes, provided all such liens shall continue until such time as they shall be discharged or foreclosed by the authority without the necessity of filing certificates of continuation, but in no event for longer that ten years. The amount of any such rate or charge which remains due and unpaid for thirty days may, with interest thereon at the same rate as unpaid taxes and with reasonable attorneys' fees, be recovered by the authority in a civil action in the name of the authority against such owners. Any municipality shall be subject to the same rate or charges under the same conditions as other users of such water supply system.

Sec. 15. (a) The representative policy board shall establish an office of consumer affairs to act as the advocate for consumer interests in all matters which may affect consumers in the district, including without limitation matters of rates, water quality and supply. The costs of such office of consumer affairs, unless otherwise provided by the state, shall be paid by the authority.

(b) The office of consumer affairs is authorized to appear and participate in any regulatory or judicial proceedings, federal or state, in which the interests of such consumers may be involved. The office of consumer affairs shall have access to the authority's records, shall be entitled to call upon the assistance of the authority's experts and shall have the benefit of all other facilities or information of the authority in carrying out the duties of the office, except for such internal documents, information or data as are not available to parties to the authority's proceedings.

(c) Nothing in this section shall be construed to prevent any party interested in any proceeding or action of the authority from appearing in person or from being represented by counsel therein. As used in this section, "consumer" means any person, company, corporation, association, city, borough or town that receives service from the authority whether or not such person, company, corporation, association, city, borough or town is financially responsible for such service.

Sec. 16. All contracts in excess of five thousand dollars for any supplies, materials, equipment, construction work or other contractual services shall be in writing and shall be awarded upon sealed bids or proposals made in compliance with a public notice duly advertised by publication at least ten days before the time fixed for opening said bids or proposals, except for contracts for professional services, when the supplies, materials, equipment or work can only be furnished by a single party or when the authority determines by a two-thirds vote of the entire authority that the award of such contract by negotiation without public bidding will be in the best interest of the authority. The authority may in its sole discretion reject all such bids or proposals or any bids received from a person, firm or corporation the authority finds to be unqualified to perform the contract, and shall award such contract to the lowest responsible bidder qualified to perform the contract.

Sec. 17. (a) If any member or employee of the representative policy board or of the authority is financially interested in or has any personal beneficial interest, directly or indirectly, in any proposed contract or proposed purchase order for any supplies, materials, equipment or contractual services to be furnished to or used by the representative policy board or the authority, such member or employee shall immediately so inform the representative policy board or the authority, whichever he is a member or employee of, and shall take no part in the deliberations or vote concerning such contract or purchase order. The representative policy board, as to its members and employees, and the authority, as to its members and employees, may terminate the membership or employment of any person who violates this subsection.

(b) No member or employee of the representative policy board or of the authority shall accept or receive, directly or indirectly, from any person, firm or corporation to which any contract or purchase order may be awarded, by rebate, gift or otherwise, any money, or any thing of value or any promise, obligation or contract for future reward compensation. Any person who violates any provision of this subsection shall be fined not more than five hundred dollars or imprisoned for not more than six months or both.

Sec. 18. (a) Notwithstanding any other provision of sections 1 to 33, inclusive, of this act, the authority shall not sell or otherwise transfer any unimproved real property or any interest or right therein, except for access or utility purposes, or develop such property for any use not directly related to a water supply function, other than for public recreational use not prohibited by section 25-43c of the general statutes, until the land use standards and disposition policies required by subsection (b) of this section have been approved by the representative policy board, unless the chief executive officer of the town or city in which such property is located has approved such sale, transfer or development in writing.

(b) Within two years from the date it acquires all or part of a water supply system, the authority shall develop and submit to the representative policy board for approval (1) standards for determining the suitability of its real property for categories of land use, including which, if any, of its real property may be surplus with regard to the purity and adequacy of both present and future water supply, which, if any, may be desirable for specified modes of recreation or open space use and which may be suitable for other uses, giving due consideration to the state plan of conservation and development, to classification and performance standards recommended in the final report of the council on water company lands pursuant to subsection (c) of section 16-49c of the general statutes and to such other plans and standards as may be appropriate and (2) policies regarding the disposition of its real property including identification of dispositions which are unlikely to have any significant effect on the environment. Prior to approving any standards or policies specified in this subsection, the representative policy board shall hold one or more public hearings to consider the proposed standards and policies. The proposed standards and policies shall be available for public inspection in the offices of the authority from the date notice of such hearing is published. The authority may amend such standards and policies from time to time with the approval of the representative policy board, which shall hold public hearings if it deems such amendments substantial.

(c) After approval of land use standards and disposition policies in the manner provided in subsection (b), the authority shall not sell or otherwise transfer any real property or any interest or right therein, except for access or utility purposes, or develop such property for any use not directly related to a water supply function, other than for public recreational use not prohibited by section 25-43c of the general statutes, without the approval of a majority of the weighted votes of all of the members of the representative policy board in the case of a parcel of twenty acres or less, and by three-fourths of the weighted votes of all of the members of said board in the case of a parcel in excess of twenty acres. The representative policy board shall not approve such sale or other transfer unless it determines, following a public hearing, that the proposed action (1) conforms to the established standards and policies of the authority, (2) is not likely to affect the environment adversely, particularly with respect to the purity and adequacy of both present and future water supply and (3) is in the public interest, giving due consideration, among other factors, to the financial impact of the proposed action on the customers of the authority and on the municipality in which the real property is located.

(d) Each request by the authority for approval pursuant to subsection (c) shall be accompanied by an evaluation of the potential impact of the proposed action for which approval is requested, which shall include: (1) A description of the real property and its environment, including its existing watershed function and the costs to the authority of maintaining such property in its current use; (2) a statement that the proposed action conforms to the land classification standards and disposition policies of the authority; (3) a detailed statement of the environmental impact of the proposed action and, if appropriate, of any alternatives to the proposed action, considering (A) direct and indirect effects upon the purity and adequacy of both present and future water supply, (B) the relationship of the proposed action to existing land use plans, including municipal and regional land use plans and the state plan of conservation and development, (C) any adverse environmental effects which cannot be avoided if the proposed action is implemented, (D) any irreversible and irretrievable commitments of resources which would be involved should the proposed action be implemented and (E) any mitigation measures proposed to minimize adverse environmental impacts; except that for a sale or transfer identified in accordance with subsection (b) as being unlikely to have any significant effect on the environment, the authority may submit a preliminary assessment of the impact likely to occur in lieu of such detailed statement of environmental impact, and the representative policy board may, on the basis of such preliminary assessment, waive or modify the requirements for such detailed statement; and (4) a summary of the final evaluation and recommendation of the authority.

(e) The representative policy board shall submit the evaluation required by subsection (d) of this section for comment and review, at least sixty days in advance of the public hearing, to the department of health, the department of planning and energy policy, the regional planning agency for the region, the chief executive officer of the city or town in which the real property is situated and other appropriate agencies, and shall make such evaluation available to the public for inspection. The decision of the representative policy board approving or disapproving the proposed action shall be published in a newspaper or newspapers having a general circulation within the district and copies of such decision shall be filed with the clerk of each town and city in the district.

(f) Whenever the authority intends to sell or otherwise transfer any unimproved real property or any interest or right therein after approval by the representative policy board, the authority shall first notify in writing, by certified mail, return receipt requested, the commissioner of environmental protection and the legislative body of the city or town in which such land is situated, of such intention to sell or otherwise transfer such property and the terms of such sale or other transfer, and no agreement to sell or otherwise transfer property may be entered into by the authority except as provided in this subsection. (1) Within ninety days after such notice has been given, the legislative body of the city or town or commissioner of environmental protection may give written notice to the authority by certified mail, return receipt requested, of the desire of the city, town or state to acquire such property and each shall have the right to acquire the interest in the property which the authority has declared its intent to sell or otherwise transfer, provided the state's right to acquire the property shall be secondary to that of the city of town. (2) If the legislative body of the city or town or the commissioner of environmental protection fails to give notice as provided in subdivision (1) or gives notice to the authority by certified mail, return receipt requested, that the city, town or state does not desire to acquire such property, the city or town or the state shall have waived its right to acquire such property in accordance with the terms of this subsection. (3) Within eighteen months after notice has been given as provided in subdivision (1) by the city or town or the state of its desire to acquire such property, the authority shall sell the property to the city or town or the state, as the case may be, or, if the parties cannot agree upon the amount to be paid therefor, the city or town or the state may proceed to acquire the property in the manner specified for redevelopment agencies in accordance with sections 8-128 to 8-1333, inclusive, of the general statutes, provided property subject to the provisions of subsections (b) and (c) of section 25-32 of the general statutes shall not be sold without the approval of the department of health. (4) If the city or town or the state fails to acquire the property or to proceed as provided as provided in said sections within eighteen months after notice has been given by the city or town or the state of its desire to acquire the property, such city or town or the state shall have waived its rights to acquire such property in accordance with the terms of this subsection. (5) Notwithstanding the provisions of section 21 of this act, the authority shall not be obligated to make payments in lieu of taxes on such property for the period from the date the city or town gives notice of its desire to acquire such property to the date it either acquires or waives its right to acquire such property. (6) Notwithstanding the provisions of subdivision (4) if the authority thereafter proposed to sell or otherwise transfer such property to any person subject to less restrictions on use or for a price less than that offered by the authority to the city or town and the state, the authority shall first notify the city or town and the commissioner of environmental protection of such proposal in the manner provided in subdivision (1), and such city or town and the state shall again have the option to acquire such property and may proceed to acquire such property in the same manner and within the same time limitations as are provided in subdivisions (1) to (4), inclusive, of this subsection. (7) The provisions of this subsection shall not apply to transfers of real property from the authority to any public service company. (8) A copy of each notice required by this subsection shall be sent by the party giving such notice to the clerk of the town or city in which the real property is situated and such clerk shall make all such notices part of the appropriate land records.

(g) Nothing contained in this section shall be construed to deprive the state department of health of its jurisdiction under section 25-32 of the general statutes. The authority shall notify the state commissioner of health of any proposed sale or other transfer of land, or change of use, as required by said section.

(h) The authority shall use the proceeds of any sale or transfer under this section solely for capital improvements to its remaining properties, acquisition of real property or any interest or right therein, retirement of debt or any combination of such purposes.

Sec. 19. The authority shall not acquire, by purchase, lease or otherwise, any existing water supply system or parts thereof or commence any project costing more than three million dollars to repair, improve, construct, reconstruct, enlarge and extend any of its properties or systems without the approval, following a public hearing, of a majority of the total weighted votes of the membership of the representative policy board. In the case of the first acquisition by the authority of an existing water supply system or part thereof, after such approval by the representative policy board the authority shall file with the town clerk of each city and town in the district its plan for such acquisition. The legislative body of each such city and town shall approve or disapprove such acquisition plan within sixty days after such filing, provided failure to disapprove within such sixty days shall be deemed approval of such acquisition plan. The authority shall not first acquire an existing water supply system or part thereof except in accordance with an acquisition plan approved by at least sixty per cent of such legislative bodies.

Sec. 20. (a) The authority shall have an annual audit of its accounts, books, and records by a certified public accountant selected by the representative policy board. A copy of the audit shall be filed in the office of the town clerk in each town within the district and with the public utilities control authority, and shall be available for public inspection during the ordinary business hours of the authority at the principal office of the authority. A concise financial statement shall be published annually, at least once, in a newspaper of general circulation in the municipality where the principal office of the authority is located. If such publication is not made by the authority, the representative policy board shall publish such statement at the expense of the authority.

(b) The attorney general may examine the books, accounts and records of the authority.

Sec. 21. (a) The authority shall not be required to pay taxes or assessments upon any of the properties acquired by it or under its jurisdiction, control or supervision or upon its activities, provided in lieu of such taxes or assessments the authority shall make annual payments to each municipality in which it owns property equal to the taxes which would otherwise be due for the property of the authority in such municipality, excluding any improvements made to or construction on any such real property by the authority, provided land owned by the authority shall be assessed in accordance with section 12-63 of the general statutes, and provided further payments for property acquired by the authority during any tax year shall be adjusted for such fractional year in accordance with the customary practice in such municipality for adjusting taxes between the buyer and seller of real property. In addition, the authority shall reimburse each such municipality for its expenses in providing municipal services to any improvements made to or constructed on any real property by the authority within such municipality. As used in this section, "improvements" does not include water pipes or improvements to water pipes.

(b) The authority may contest the assessed valuation of any properties owned by the authority with respect to which any payment in lieu of taxes is determined in the same manner as any owner of real property in such municipality.

(c) In the event the authority in any year does not have sufficient funds to make such payments in lieu of taxes, or any portion of them, as the same become due and payable, the authority shall adjust its rates and charges and the representative policy board shall approve such rates and charges, in the manner provided in section 14 of this act, so as to provide funds within one year after the date on which such payment became due and payable to make such payment. Any municipality aggrieved by the failure of the authority to make any payment in lieu of taxes or portion thereof as the same becomes due and payable may apply to the superior court for the county in which such municipality is situated for an order directing the authority to appropriately increase its rates and charges.

Sec. 22. (a) The authority, subject to the approval of the representative policy board, shall have the power and is authorized from time to time to issue its negotiable bonds for any of its corporate purposes, including incidental expenses in connection therewith, and to secure the payment of the same by a lien or pledge covering all or part of its contracts, earnings or revenues. The authority shall have power from time to time, whenever it deems refunding expedient, to refund any bonds by the issuance of new bonds within the terms of any refunding provisions of its bonds, whether the bonds to be refunded have or have not matured, and may issue bonds partly to refund bonds then outstanding and partly for any of its public purposes. Except as may be otherwise expressly provided by the authority, every issue of bonds by the authority shall be preferred obligations, taking priority over all other claims against the authority, including payments in lieu of taxes to any municipality, and payable out of any moneys, earnings or revenues of the authority, subject only to any agreements with the holders of particular bonds pledging any particular moneys, earnings or revenues. Notwithstanding the fact that the bonds may be payable from a special fund, if they are otherwise of such form and character as to be negotiable instruments under the terms of the uniform commercial code, the bonds shall be negotiable instruments within the meaning of and for all purposes of the uniform commercial code, subject only to the provisions of the bonds for registration.

(b) The bonds shall be authorized by resolution of the authority and shall bear such date or dates, mature at such time or times, not exceeding forty years from their receptive dates, bear interest at such rates per annum, not exceeding statutory limitations, be payable at such times, be in such denomination, be in such form, either coupon or registered, carry such registration privileges, be executed in such manner, be payable in lawful money of the United States of America, at such place or places, and be subject to such terms of redemption as such resolution or resolutions may provide. All bonds of the authority shall be sold through a negotiated sale or a public sale upon sealed bids to the bidder who shall offer the lowest net interest cost to the authority, to be determined by the authority. The notice of sale shall be published at least once, not less than ten or more than forty days before the date of sale, in a financial newspaper circulated in the state of Connecticut and the city of New York and designated by the authority. The notice shall call for the receipt of sealed bids and shall fix the date, time and place of sale.

(c) Any resolution or resolutions authorizing any bonds or any issue of bonds may contain provisions which shall be a part of the contract with the holders of the bonds thereby authorized as to (1) pledging all or any part of the moneys, earnings, income and revenues derived from all or any part of the properties of the authority to secure the payment of the bonds or of any issue of the bonds subject to such agreement with the bondholders as may then exist; (2) the rates, rentals, fees and other charges to be fixed and collected and the amounts to be raised in each year thereby, and the use and disposition of the earnings and other revenues; (3) the setting aside of reserves and the creation of sinking funds and the regulation and disposition thereof; (4) limitations on the right of authority to restrict and regulate the use of the properties in connection with which such bonds are issued; (5) limitations on the purposes to which, and the manner in which, the proceeds of sale of any issue of bonds may be applied; (6) limitations on the issuance of additional bonds, the terms upon which additional bonds may be issued and secured, and the refunding of outstanding or other bonds; (7) the procedure, if any, by which the terms of any contract with bondholders may be amended or abrogated, the amount of bonds the holders of which must consent thereto and the manner in which such consent may be given; (8) the creation of special funds into which any earnings or revenues of the authority may be deposited; (9) the terms and provisions of any trust deed or indenture securing the bonds or under which bonds may be issued; (10) definitions of the acts or omission to act which shall constitute a default in the obligations and duties of the authority to the bondholders and providing the rights and remedies of the bondholders in the event of such default, including as a matter of right the appointment of a receiver, provided such rights and remedies shall not be inconsistent with the general laws of this site; (11) limitations on the power of the authority to sell or otherwise dispose of its properties; (12) any other matters, of like or different character, which in any way affect the security or protection of the bonds; and (13) limitations on the amount of moneys derived from the properties to be expended for operating, administrative or other expenses of the authority.

(d) It is the intention of the general assembly that any pledge of earnings, revenues or other moneys made by the authority shall be valid and binding from the time when the pledge is made; that the earnings, revenues or other moneys so pledged and thereafter received by the authority shall immediately be subject to the lien of such pledge without any physical delivery thereof or further act, and that the lien of any such pledge be valid and binding as against all parties having claims of any kind in tort, contract or otherwise against the authority irrespective of whether such parties have notice thereof. Neither the resolution nor any other instrument by which a pledge is created need be recorded.

(e) Neither the members of the authority nor any person executing the bonds shall be liable personally on the bonds or be subject to any personal liability or accountability by reason of the issuance thereof.

(f) The authority shall have the power out of any funds available to purchase as distinguished from the power of redemption above provided, any bonds issued by it at a price of not more than the principal amount thereof and accrued interest, and all bonds so purchased shall be canceled.

(g) In the discretion of the authority, the bonds may be secured by a trust indenture by and between the authority and a corporate trustee, which may be any trust company or bank having the powers of a trust company. Such trust indenture may contain such provisions for protecting and enforcing the rights and remedies of the bondholders as may be reasonable and proper and not in violation if any law, including covenants setting forth the duties of the authority in relation to the construction, maintenance, operation, repair and insurance of the properties and the custody, safeguarding and application of all moneys, and may provide that the properties shall be constructed and paid for under the supervision and approval of consulting engineers. The authority may provide by such trust indenture or other depository for the methods of disbursement thereof, with such safeguards and restrictions as it may determine. All expenses incurred in carrying out such trust indenture may be treated as part of the cost of maintenance, operation and repair of the properties. If the bonds are secured by a trust indenture, bondholders shall have no authority to appoint a separate trustee to represent them.

(h) Notwithstanding any other provisions of sections 1 to 33, inclusive, of this act, any resolution or resolutions authorizing bonds or notes of the authority shall contain a covenant by the authority that it will at all times maintain rates, fees, rentals or other charges sufficient to pay, and that any contracts entered into by the authority for the sale and distribution of water shall contain rates, fees, rentals or other charges sufficient to pay, the cost of operation and maintenance of the properties and the principal of and interest on any obligation issued pursuant to such resolution or resolutions as the same severally become due and payable, and to maintain any reserves or other funds required by the terms of such resolution or resolutions.

(i) If any officer of the authority whose signature or a facsimile of whose signature appears on any bonds or coupons ceases to be such officer before delivery of such bonds, such signature or such facsimile shall nevertheless be valid and sufficient for all purposes as if he had remained in office until such delivery.

Sec. 23. The authority shall have the power and is authorized to issue negotiable bond anticipation notes and may renew the same from time to time, but the maximum maturity of any such note, including renewals thereof, shall not exceed five years from date of such original note. Such note shall be paid from any moneys of the authority available therefor and not otherwise pledged or from the proceeds of the sale of the bonds of the authority in anticipation of which they were issued. The notes shall be issued in the same manner as the bonds and such notes and the resolution or resolutions authorizing such notes may contain any provisions, conditions or limitations which the bonds or a bond resolution of the authority may contain. Such notes shall be fully negotiable as the bonds of the authority.

Sec. 24. The state of Connecticut does pledge to and agree with the holders of the bonds or notes of the authority that the state will not limit or alter the rights vested in the authority to acquire, construct, maintain, operate, reconstruct and improve the properties, to establish and collect the revenues, rates, rentals, fees and other charges referred to in sections 1 to 33, inclusive, of this act and to fulfill the terms of any agreements made with the holders of the bonds or notes, or in any way impair the rights and remedied of the bondholders or noteholders until the bonds or notes together with interest thereon, interest on any unpaid installments of interest and all costs and expenses in connection with any action or proceeding by or on behalf of the bondholders or noteholders are fully met and discharged.

Sec. 25. The bonds, notes or other obligations of the authority shall not be a debt of the state of Connecticut or of any municipality, and neither the state nor any municipality shall be liable therefor, nor shall they be payable out of funds other than those of the authority.

Sec. 26. The bonds and notes of the authority shall be securities in which all public officers and bodies of this state and all municipalities, all insurance companies and associations and other persons carrying on an insurance business, all banks, bankers, trust companies, savings banks, savings and loan associations, investment companies and other persons whatever, except as hereinafter provided, who are now or may be authorized to invest in bonds or other obligations of the state, may properly and legally invest funds, including capital in their control or belonging to them: provided, notwithstanding the provisions of any other general statute or special act to the contrary, such bonds shall not be eligible for the investment of funds, including capital, of trusts, estates or guardianships under the control of individual administrators, guardians, executors, trustees or other individual fiduciaries. The bonds shall also be securities which may be deposited with and may be received by all public officers and bodies of this state and all municipalities and municipal subdivisions for any purpose for which the deposit of bonds or other obligations of this state is now or may be authorized.

Sec. 27. The state of Connecticut covenants with the purchasers and with all subsequent holders and transferees of bonds or notes issued by the authority, in consideration of the acceptance of and payment for the bonds or notes, that the bonds and notes of the authority, the income therefrom and all moneys, funds and revenues pledged to pay or secure the payment of such bonds or notes shall at all times be free from taxation.

Sec. 28. Nothing in sections 1 to 33, inclusive, of this act shall be construed to deprive the commissioner of environmental protection, the commissioner of health or any successor commissioner or board of any jurisdiction which such commissioners or boards may now or thereafter have. Neither the public utilities control authority nor any successor board or commissioner shall have jurisdiction of any kind over the authority, the representative policy board or the rates fixed or charges collected by the authority. The authority shall annually file the report required of municipalities pursuant to section 16-29 of the general statutes with the public utility control authority and the clerks of the towns and cities within the district.

Sec. 29. Insofar as the provisions of sections 1 to 33, inclusive, of this act are inconsistent with the provisions of any other general or special act or any municipal ordinance, the provisions of sections 1 to 33, inclusive, of this act shall be controlling; providing nothing contained in sections 1 to 33, inclusive, of this act shall exempt the authority from compliance with zoning regulations lawfully established by any municipality, except that the plants, structures and other facilities of the water supply system owned or operated by the authority shall be permitted uses in all zoning districts in every city, town or borough within the district; and provided further that that authority may not construct purification or filtration plants in any zoning district in which such use is not permitted under local zoning regulations without first obtaining approval of the proposed location of such facility from the representative policy board following a public hearing.

Sec. 30. (a) A person who is aggrieved by a decision of the representative policy board with respect to the establishment of rates or charges, the sale or other transfer or change of use of real property, the location of purification or filtration plants, the commencement of any project costing more that three million dollars to repair, improve, construct, reconstruct, enlarge or extend any of the properties or systems of the authority or the acquisition by purchase, lease or otherwise of any existing water supply system or part thereof, other than the purchase of all or any part of the properties and franchises of the New Haven Water Company, is entitled to judicial review under this section.

(b) Proceedings for review shall be instituted by filing a petition in the court of common pleas for New Haven County within thirty days after publication of the decision of the representative policy board or, if a rehearing is requested, within thirty days after the decision thereon. Copies of the petition shall be served upon the representative policy board and published in a newspaper or newspapers having general circulation in each town or city comprising the district.

(c) The filing of the petition shall not itself stay enforcement of the decision of the representative policy board. The representative policy board may grant, or the reviewing court may order, a stay upon appropriate terms, provided enforcement of a decision respecting the establishment of rates or charges may be stayed only after issuance of a judgment for the appellant by the reviewing court.

(d) Within thirty days after service of the petition, or within such further time as may be allowed by the court, the representative policy board shall transmit to the reviewing court the original or a certified copy of the entire record of the proceeding under review, which shall include the representative policy board's findings of fact and conclusions of law, separately stated. By stipulation of all parties to review the proceedings, the record may be shortened. A party unreasonably refusing to stipulate to limit the record may be taxed by the court for the additional costs. The court may require or permit subsequent corrections or additions to the record.

(e) If, before the date set for hearing, application is made to the court for leave to present additional evidence, and it is shown to the satisfaction of the court the additional evidence is material and that there were good reasons for failure to present it in the proceeding before the representative policy board, the court may refer the case back the board with instructions to make such evidence as the court directs. The representative policy board may modify its findings and decision by reason of the additional evidence and shall file that evidence and any modifications, new findings, or decisions with the reviewing court.

(f) The review shall be conducted by the court without a jury and shall be confined to the record. In cases of alleged irregularities in procedure before the representative policy board, not shown in the record, proof thereon may be taken in the court. The court, upon request, shall hear oral argument and receive written briefs.

(g) The court shall not substitute its judgment for that of the representative policy board as to the weight of the evidence on questions of fact. The court may affirm the decision of the representative policy board or remand the case for further proceedings.

The court may reverse or modify the decision if substantial rights of the appellant have been prejudiced because the findings, inferences, conclusions, or decisions are: (1) In violation of constitutional provisions, the general statutes or the provisions of this or another special act; (2) in excess of the authority of the representative policy board; (3) made upon unlawful procedure; (4) affected by other error of law; (5) clearly erroneous in view of the reliable probative, and substantial evidence on the whole record; or (6) arbitrary or capricious or characterized by abuse of discretion or clearly unwarranted exercise of discretion.

(h) In any case in which an aggrieved party claims that he cannot pay the costs of an appeal under this section and will thereby be deprived of a right to which he is entitled, he shall, within the time permitted for filing the appeal, file with the clerk of the court to which the appeal is to be taken an application for waiver of payment of such fees, costs and necessary expenses, including the requirements of bond, if any. The application shall conform to the requirements of section 28A of the Practice Book. After such hearing as the court determines is necessary, the court shall enter its judgment on the application, which judgment shall contain a statement of the facts the court has found, with its conclusions thereon. The filing of application for the waiver shall toll the time limits for the filing of an appeal until such time as a judgment on such application is entered.

(i) Neither the authority nor the representative policy board shall be construed to be an agency within the scope of chapter 54 of the general statutes.

Sec. 31. (a) Whenever the authority acquires the property and franchises of any private water company or companies operating a water supply system within its district, all employees of such company or companies who are necessary for the operation of the authority, except senior managerial officers, shall become employees of the authority and shall be credited by the authority with all rights that have accrued as of the date of such acquisition with respect to seniority, sick leave, vacation, insurance and pension benefits in accordance with the records, personnel policies or labor agreements of the acquired company or companies.

(b) The authority shall assume and observe all accrued pension obligations of such acquired company or companies, and members and beneficiaries of any pension or retirement system or other benefits established by the acquired company or companies shall continued to have such rights, privileges, benefits, obligations and status with respect to such established systems as have accrued as of the date of such acquisition. The authority may enter into agreements with representatives of its employees relative to the inclusion of its employees in any applicable state or municipal employee's retirement plan or plans. The authority may enter into agreements with representatives of its employees relative to the transfer to or the establishment of pension trust funds under the joint control of such authority and representatives of its employees, and shall have all powers necessary to maintain and administer such trust funds jointly with representatives of its employees.

(c) The authority shall assume and observe all labor contracts of such company or companies in existence at the time of transfer and all obligations incurred by such contracts regarding wages, salaries, hours, sick leave and other leave, working conditions, grievance procedures, collective bargaining and pension or retirement.

(d) The authority shall assume and observe personnel policies of such company or companies in existence at the time of transfer relating to personnel not covered by labor contracts, and all obligations incurred through such personnel policies regarding wages, salaries, hours, sick leave, vacation, pension and retirement, subject to such modifications therein as the authority may subsequently adopt, provided such modifications shall not affect any rights of such employees which have vested prior to such modification.

(e) Nothing in this section shall prevent the authority from hiring any senior managerial officers of such company on such terms as it may determine or be construed to prohibit the authority from exercising the normal prerogatives of management with respect to such matters as the promotion, demotion, assignment, transfer or discharge of its employees, nor shall the authority be bound by any terms of any personnel policy entered into by such company or companies in anticipation of acquisition by the authority.

Sec. 32. The relations between the authority and its employees with respect to collective bargaining and the arbitration of labor disputes shall be governed by sections 7-467 to 7-477, inclusive, of the general statutes.

Sec. 33. The state bond commission may insure in the name of the state and may take advance commitments to insure any sums borrowed by the authority, not exceeding in the aggregate five million dollars, for the purpose of providing working capital and organizational funds for the authority. In the event the state becomes liable as a result of default with respect of default with respect to any such sums borrowed by the authority which were so insured by the state, necessary payment shall be made by the state treasurer from funds appropriated for debt service. Whatever sums are borrowed by the authority under the provisions of this section shall be repaid to the lender or lenders of the same on or before July 1, 1988.

Sec. 34. The department of planning and energy policy, in cooperation with the public utilities control authority and the department of environmental protection, shall study and make recommendations concerning (1) the short and long term economic impact on water companies of the sale of water company owned lands and (2) construction requirements for conventional and advanced treatment facilities. Said department shall report to the governor and the general assembly no later than December 1, 1978. Said report shall include recommendations of possible forms of financial assistance for the water companies for the construction of treatment facilities, such as low interest loans, state guaranteed bonds and tax exemptions.

Sec. 35. The sum of ten thousand dollars is appropriated to the department of planning and energy policy, from the sum appropriated to the finance advisory committee, under section 1 of special act 77-46, for 1977 acts without appropriations, to carry out the purposes of section 34 of this act.

Vetoed July 14, 1977
Repassed July 25, 1977
SPECIAL ACT 77-98

Special Act Veto Message

I am returning herewith, without my approval, Special Act No. 77-98, Substitute House Bill No. 7958, "An Act Concerning Financial Assistance For Water Companies For Construction of Treatment Facilities and Creating The South Central Connecticut Regional Water Authority."

This bill would establish the South Central Connecticut Regional Water District and Authority. In addition, the bill would authorize a study of the sale of water company lands, and the potential need for financial assistance to water companies constructing treatment facilities.

The concept of a regional water authority in South Central Connecticut is a sound one. This legislation, however, does not provide adequate controls over the growth and development of this authority. The bill empowers the authority to incorporate additional towns into the water district without legislative approval, leaving open the possibility of uncontrolled expansion detrimental to the interests of the region's residents. Without these controls, the creation of a regional water authority in South Central Connecticut may be counter-productive.

The bill also grants the water authority tax exempt status, which would result in an estimated loss of state revenues in excess of one million dollars annually. In addition, the legislation authorizes the state to insure sums borrowed by the authority, not exceeding in the aggregate five million dollars. Thus, even though the project receives this support and guaranty, there is no opportunity for state involvement to oversee the development of the water authority. The absence of state participation seems contrary to the best interests of the taxpayers of Connecticut.

Therefore, I do not approve Substitute House Bill No. 7958.
Vetoed July 14, 1977, REPASSED July 25, 1977
...END...

Appendix F
Newspaper Feature Articles

Lake Saltonstall In Its Heyday Was An Oasis For Tired City Dwellers

Editor's Note: This article, in praise of Lake Saltonstall, was written by Mrs. Henry Townsend, one of many on the New Haven area who mourn the passing of the lake from a public resort to a public water supply.

With the recent closing of Lake Saltonstall to fishing by the New Haven Water Co., the public loses its last touch with this lovely lake, once a popular summer resort.

In 1890 throngs of New Haveners, seeking relief from the city's heat and in pursuit of woodland pleasures, took the 15-minute ride on the twice-daily Shoreline Railroad to the East Haven depot and then walked over to Lake Saltonstall. Here they found a comfortable refreshment house and waiting room, appropriately named "Lake View," and a dock where the boats could be hired for fishing and rowing at 10 to 50 cents an hour. The entire length of the lake (four and one half miles and "one of the loveliest sheets of water in the world") could be traveled round-trip in the little steamer, Cygnet, captained by G. Herbert Baldwin, for only 25 cents.

At the head of the lake, the passengers disembarked at the steamboat landing into a beautiful wooden picnic area called "Glen Grove," where a pavilion stood complete with tables and seats. Those family groups, parties of friends and Sunday school classes who made the trip were lavish in praise of the beauty and quiet of the incomparable Lake Saltonstall."

A MAGNIFICENT VIEW

In the *Journal and Courier*, July 16, 1892, a writer extolled the picturesque scenery which "reminds one strongly of the palisades of the Hudson." On the west side of the lake rose a sharp ridge of 250 feet, heavily wooded with pine, birch, hemlock, beech and cedar and providing at "Eagle's Nest" Point a magnificent view of the surrounding countryside: Long Island Sound, New Haven Harbor, the hills of Meriden and all the shoreline towns, snugged into the thick greenery with white church steeples poking through.

On the eastern side, verdant pastures and fields rimmed the lake's edge with particularly charming spots named: "Chestnut Grove," "Wigwam Grove," "Stillwater Bay" and "Lily Pond" (abounding in blueish-pink water lilies brought from Cape Cod). With the afternoon shadows of the high-walled hills falling early on the lake and with cool breezes gently fanning the deep (112 feet), crystal-clear waters, it is not hard to imagine why city dwellers found this park a delightful retreat. Admirers even boasted that mosquitoes were non-existent here!

Long before this scene of wild beauty was known to pleasure seekers, back in the dim days of Indian dominion, an ancient legend told of the creation of the lake. When Chief Momaugin sold his tribe's rights in the land to the English settlers, he recalled this legend: it seems the great spirit of the red man foresaw the coming of the white man and anticipating the fate of his children, his tears flowed heavily down the mountainside and scooped out the depression forming the lovely lake. "Tear of the Great Spirit" the Indians called it, or Lake Lomotonquat.

Time rolled tranquilly by with only local fishermen frequenting the "remote" lake, selling confectionery, bottled temperance drinks and ice cream, also providing plates and cutlery for the convenience of those on picnics. Walks and carriage drives encircling the lake were laid out and developed with enchanting views exposed along the way.

AN EXCITING CHANGE

But in 1890 Lake Saltonstall was in for an exciting change. By that time George H. Townsend of East Haven had acquired much of the lake property, thus satisfying a lifelong desire of his, and he had great plans to open the charms of the lake to everyone. During the next few years, the 700-acre private park began to vie successfully with the attractions offered by the better-known Savin Rock.

The grounds at Glen Grove were enlarged to include tennis and croquet courts, baseball and football fields. Andrew Granniss of Foxon opened up a refreshment saloon there, selling confectionery, bottled temperance drinks and ice cream, also providing plates and cutlery for the convenience of those on picnics. Walks and carriage drives encircling the lake were laid out and developed with enchanting views exposed along the way.

But the biggest allurement of the lake was the superb fishing. Perch, pickerel, bullheads, roach and crappies (a very gamey fish 4 to 5 pounds when mature) kept the most eager anglers busy all day. The first black bass ever known in these waters were brought here from Winsted in 1858 by George Townsend, who continued to stock the lake at an average of 2,000 fish per year. He also

Saltonstall, the barge Governor Saltonstall and the handsome launch Electric, straight from the New Haven Street Railway Co., who said: "I do not know what the water company intends to do, but I hope it will not shut the public off from one of New Haven's finest summer resorts."

Such was the great upsurge in popularity of this new resort that many talked of building large summer hotels and vacation cottages on the lake's edge and converting the mountain into a huge park. And it wasn't only in summer that the lake drew the public. In winter many skaters, young and old, flocked to the lake for a day of sliding and gliding. On Jan. 6, 1895, 2,000 skaters were reported out on the ice with the railroad running a special train to accommodate the crowds.

June 22, 1870, Lake Saltonstall was the site of a gallant rowing contest over a three-mile course between Harvard and Yale's scientific schools crews, Lawrence and Granniss Four Corners was extended to East Haven Green and then to Lake Saltonstall, the rush was on in earnest. The cars, leaving every 20 minutes, were packed with people who looked forward for a respite from the hot, dusty city. "A GREAT DAY AT LAKE SALTONSTALL" headlined *The Daily Palladium* on May 31, 1895. "BEAT ALL RECORDS!" The newspaper continued: "A moderate estimate of those who spent a part of the day at Saltonstall would be 3,000." Extra excursion boats were added to the little fleet: the steamer Susie

stocked the streams with trout fry and made deep, little pools for them by damming the streams at frequent intervals.

TROLLEY BOOM

In the summer of 1894, when the electric street car or trolley line from New Haven Green to Granniss Four Corners was extended to East Haven Green and then to Lake Saltonstall, the rush was on in earnest. The cars, leaving every 20 minutes, were packed with people who looked forward for a respite from the hot, dusty city. "A GREAT DAY AT LAKE SALTONSTALL" headlined *The Daily Palladium* on May 31, 1895. "BEAT ALL RECORDS!" The newspaper continued: "A moderate estimate of those who spent a part of the day at Saltonstall would be 3,000." Extra excursion boats were added to the little fleet: the steamer Susie

All of this public enjoyment came to an abrupt end in June 1895 when the New Haven Water Co., bought the surrounding land—in the words of Eli Whitney, Jr., President: "to keep the water in a pure condition and prevent its contamination by being used for pleasure purposes."

This causes much consternation among the excursionists, none more so than General Manager Dodge of the New Haven Street Railway Co., who

Lake Saltonstall railroad station and steamboat landing.

The merits of the resort were much publicized in the newspapers. *The Shore Line Times*, May 18, 1894: "Lake Saltonstall is destined to be one of the most attractive spots in the state, if it is not already." *Meriden Daily Republican*, Feb. 20, 1895: "One of the most beautiful summer resorts in the state is Lake Saltonstall." *The Evening Leader*, June 14, 1894: "Pretty Lake Saltonstall—the heart of the Adirondacks furnishes no wider or more enchanting resting places for our tourists."

All was not lost immediately however; the public still retained the right to fish with a permit from the water company. But finally in March 1966 the last fateful blow was struck, CLOSED TO FISHING! PUBLIC KEEP OUT! TRESPASSERS WILL BE PROSECUTED! the signs might read. The tears of ardent fishermen might well mingle with the tears of the Indians' great spirit.

So now lovely Lake Saltonstall reverts to its original state of quiet woods and serene waters. Time marches on—or

FORUM

NO HANDOUTS FOR WATER COMPANY

DOROTHY McCLUSKEY

Why does *The Register* in its recent editorial (Dec. 15) call for financial relief from the General Assembly for the New Haven Water Company when this firm has repeatedly misled both the public and it stockholders in attempting to solve its capital financing needs?

First, the New Haven Water Company has already obtained special assistance from the General Assembly to help it negotiate public ownership, yet it had rejected three generous purchase offers from the public. Secondly, the water company is misleading its stockholders about both its right and its ability to sell large tracts of its watershed land.

In 1975 when I first introduced legislation to establish a regional water authority in the New Haven area, the proposal failed to pass. Two years later I was successful in convincing my colleagues that purchase of the New Haven Water Company by a regional authority would benefit both consumers and the affected communities by keeping water rates down for consumers and by protecting the tax base and providing a voice for area towns in the water utility management.

The legislature supported creation of the South Central Connecticut Regional Water Authority with the clear understanding that the water company was in fact for sale at a fairly negotiated price.

Let's look more closely at the fairness of the purchase offers, one from the authority and two from the city of New Haven. The most recent and highest of the three offers, is at a price that will give the stockholders approximately double the book value of each outstanding share of common stock, an astonishingly generous offer on any businessman's opinion!

By rejecting this latest and final offer, the water company's Board of Directors in effect makes a mockery of the months of hard work and good faith negotiations and compromise undertaken by the City of New Haven and the authority representatives. By rejecting the potential windfall profits of this offer, the Board of Directors is forcing the public to ask if the water company has ever really been for sale or if the Board of Directors had deliberately misled its shareholders and the legislature.

Let's also look at the land sales that the Board of Directors offers as a panacea for the company's difficulty in financing filtration plant construction. According to Department of Environmental Protection records, the New Haven Water Company is the only water utility in the state of Connecticut that plans to sell its watershed lands.

In proposing massive land sales the company is ignoring—even defying—a new state law and moratorium restricting land sales. In fact the directors seem to brush off the state law as a legal impediment that their attorneys will overcome.

However, the U.S. Supreme Court, on Dec. 4, upheld both the moratorium and Connecticut's right to restrict water company land sales in order to protect public health. In light of this decision, it is evident the directors may have great difficulty in selling all the land that they assure their stockholders they can.

Buy why promote watershed land sale at all when in fact it is doubtful, even without state restrictions,

that the sale could bring sufficient revenue to solve the water company's financial problems? Could it be that the Board of Directors is using the threat if massive land sales as a form of blackmail over area communities in order to still further escalate the public purchase offers?

The whole proposed land sale deal typifies the cavalier attitude that the Board of Directors has taken toward the public. Scarcely a week goes by that the media does not report irreversible contamination of a water supply in Connecticut or other states from some previously unsuspected source of pollution. If the lands now protecting our water supply reservoirs were sold, what assurance do we have that the same thing won't happen here? I find it difficult to accept the implication that the Board of Directors' greed has blinded it to the possibility its watershed land sales proposals could jeopardize the health of area residents.

Given the record of irresponsibility, why should the General Assembly help the New Haven Water Company? There is absolutely no justification for the legislature to give a handout, at taxpayer expense, to a water utility that has repeatedly turned down the opportunity to help itself.

Dorothy McCluskey, state representative from the 86th District, representing North Branford and the eastern part of Wallingford, is chairman of a subcommittee on water company lands and sponsor of legislation enabling creation of the South Central Connecticut Regional Water Authority and regulating the sale of public water supply lands.

WHO IS IT THAT'S
MISLEADING THE PUBLIC?

An open letter from the New Haven Water Company to Mrs. Dorothy McCluskey, state representative from the 86th District, representing North Branford and the eastern part of Wallingford.

Dear Mrs. McCluskey,

After our Board of Directors rejected an offer from the City of New Haven to buy the Water Company for $107 million, or $89 per share ($84.76 based on current shares), there was considerable reaction to this decision in the news media, principally the New Haven Register.

There were comments by Mayor Frank Logue and other public officials, a large ad in the Register and Journal Courier, paid for by the family of the late Joel Cohn, interviews in the Register and on radio and TV, and an article written by you in the December 21 issue of the Register, entitled "No Handouts for the Water Company."

As often happens in such cases, some of the remarks were heated and intemperate, and some were misleading, and some were blatantly false.

People who are unfamiliar with the background preceding the City offer can perhaps be excused for misstatements made in the heat of emotion or disappointment.

NO EXCUSE FOR DISTORTIONS

But in our opinion there can be no excuse for the distortions that appear in your article. As chairman of the sub-committee on water company lands, as sponsor of legislation which created the South Central Connecticut Regional Water and as the author of legislation which controls the sale of water utility land, you should be fully informed on all aspects of this issue.

Furthermore, as an elected representative to the State Legislature, you bear an additional responsibility to be honest and accurate in your statements. In your article, you accuse us of "repeatedly" misleading both the public and our stockholders "attempting to solve capital financing needs."

Is it possible, Mrs. McCluskey, that you and not the Water Company, may be misleading the public?

You say, for example, that we have rejected "three generous purchase offers" which you describe as fair. On what basis do you call them "generous" and "fair," both of which are relative terms?

If you (and the City) really think that $89 per share ($84.76 based on current shares) is a fair offer, why don't you publicly support a proposal that the City exercise its option so that the purchase price can be decided by the courts or by third party arbitration?

Is it because you fear that any arbitrated price (which would be binding on the City and the Regional Authority) as well as the Water Company) might be higher than the $89 offer?

OUR POSITION HAS ALWAYS BEEN CLEAR

Our position on any offer to buy the Water Company has been very clear and publicly stated from the beginning of the negotiations, including several times in your presence. We have said that we could not support any offer if we believed that the stockholders could benefit to a greater extent under continued private ownership. And we have never said that we would sell at whatever the highest offer was.

You refer to the moratorium on land sales (legislation in which you were a principal author) and say that "directors may have great difficulty in selling all the land they assure their stockholders they can."

Just who this is misleading whom, Mrs. McCluskey? The facts, as you well know but have chosen not to disclose, are that the moratorium on watershed land sales expires next June and

even now does not restrict the sale of non-watershed lands.

We are therefore able to sell approximately 5,000 acres of Class 3 (non-watershed) land in the next several years. Both the State Health Department and the Land Study Council have agreed that most non-watershed land can be disposed of without injury to the water supply. We have repeatedly said that we are willing to work with the towns on a land disposal program.

PROTECTING WATERSHED LAND

With respect to the Class 2 lands now under moratorium until June of 1979, we fully recognize that nature of that property and the restrictions under which it must be disposed of to fully protect the water supply. So you see, Mrs. McCluskey, we aren't ignoring or defying any laws even though we think some of them (see below) are absurd.

Protecting surplus watershed land from improper use in the event of its sale is a thoroughly laudable objective and one which we support 100%. We would support efforts to go even further and protect all watershed land, whether we own it or not. However, let's look at what some of your restrictive legislation has accomplished.

For one thing, it prohibits us from selling our former operations center on Skiff Street in Hamden, which we occupied for nearly 25 years before consolidating Water Company operations at Sargent Drive in New Haven.

Your legislation apparently prohibits us from selling the building (valued at approximately $750,000) even if we maintain ownership of the land on which its built, because whoever moves in might "endanger" the water supply.

Let's examine the absurdity of this reason. Of the entire Lake Whitney watershed, some 3% is owned by the Water Company and the other 97% is in private hands. The water runoff into Mill River (which feed Lake Whitney where the water is filtered and treated) is from areas such as the Hamden Mart, Hamden Plaza, Dixwell Avenue, Whitney Avenue, and the rest of Skiff Street, a total of 36 square miles.

Compared to these areas, the water runoff from our tiny complex on Skiff Street is hardly measurable. Yet under your legislation, we cannot sell our building even with restrictions as to use and even if we continue as owners of the land—because in some unspecified way it might pose a "danger" to the water supply.

Ridiculous, isn't it?

If we are unable to lease that building or find another productive use for it, should the rate-payers be burdened with the cost of keeping it to "project" the water supply, when continued ownership provides no significant added protection?

ABOUT "IRREVERSIBLE CONTAMINATION"

Your article says that scarcely a week goes by without reports of "irreversible contamination of a water supply in Connecticut or other states from some previously unsuspected source of pollution." You asked what assurance the public has that the same thing won't happen here.

Please don't confuse us with small community water supplies. We've been in business for over 130 years with no "irreversible contamination" of our water supplies. In fact, even at Lake Whitney where, as we've said, we own only 3% of the watershed, we're able to provide quality water through watershed monitoring, testing and mechanical filtration. If an intensely developed area like Lake Whitney region can be efficiently managed to avoid jeopardizing the water supply, then out other surface water reservoirs, which will also be filtered, will be even better protected, since we will maintain ownership of all the essential watershed land (certainly more than 3%) and the rest of the land will be disposed of with restrictions as to use.

Through some obscure reasoning, you seem to find this "irresponsible" and say that we are a water utility that has "repeatedly turned down the offer to help itself."

Once again, Mrs. McCluskey, your statements mislead the public. Let's take a look at how we have very much helped

ourselves—and a lot of other people along the way, including an attempt to help your own North Branford townspeople.

HOW WE HAVE HELPED OURSELVES

1. As early as 1972 we led the fight for Connecticut Development Authority "pass-through" financing of filter plants at tax-free rates, a plan that will save ratepayers millions of dollars in interest charges. Through our efforts and the cooperation of the legislature, this technique is now benefiting consumers.

2. We were one of the leaders in the fight to convince the Public Utilities Control Authority that construction work-in-progress should be included for rate-making purposes for filter plants necessary under requirements of the Safe Drinking Water Act. That policy is now recognized by the PUCA, a giant step forward for all Connecticut water utilities and their customers.

3. We have shown several towns, including your hometown of North Branford, how they could acquire the bulk of excess Water Company land holdings within their town boundaries without raising taxes. North Branford could buy a substantial amount of Water Company land by using the extra tax revenue we will be paying when our multi-million dollar filter plant is built. In other words, North Branford and the other towns would be able to own Water Company land and pay for it with Water Company dollars.

How's that for helping ourselves, Mrs. McCluskey—and trying to help the towns, too?

However, you have chosen not to support this type of plan, preferring instead to sponsor legislation which could require us to keep land we no longer need, which our customers must support through their rates.

Do you really believe that this is in the long-term best interest of North Branford and our region?

4. You seem to be unaware of how we have helped ourselves (as well as our customers) with an innovative plan which will allow us to support the $112 million construction program

necessary in the next decade to comply with the Safe Drinking Water Act.

Through our efforts in obtaining Connecticut Development Authority participation, we have been able to achieve low-cost debt financing.

Through our persistence on seeking recognition for the costs of construction work-in-progress, we have made construction of the filter plants feasible.

And to help ourselves in the equity area, we have formulated a plan which would permit us to dispose of our surplus land holdings during the next 15 to 20 years, plow all of the proceeds back into the company and thus provide the equity investment to balance the debt investment.

With this publicly announced plan, how can you say we "turn down the opportunity to help ourselves," Mrs. McCluskey?

The sequence of your legislature activities appears to suggest your motives. First you author a bill which restricts land sales by a water company.

You then introduce legislation which creates a public organization empowered to buy the New Haven Water Company. When our Board turns down an offer from the City (which is to be passed along to the Regional Authority) as insufficient, you tell us the offer is fair because we can't sell all of our land. Why? Because of your legislation. A neat power play, Mrs. McCluskey!

In closing, we'd just like to say that in the future we hope you'll think twice before you accuse us of misleading the public.

New Haven Water

90 Sargent Drive New Haven, Connecticut

161

BIBLIOGRAPHY

We list here the writings and meetings that have been most useful in writing this book. This bibliography is not a complete record of all the works and sources we have consulted. We have drawn heavily upon our personal participation in the events recorded here.

We have enjoyed the complete cooperation of the administration and staff of the Regional Water Authority with free access to records, correspondence and memoranda. The Minute Books of the Authority, the Representative Policy Board and the New Haven Water Company Board of Directors were used extensively. The Connecticut General Assembly's Office of Fiscal Analysis and Office of Legislative Research were invaluable resources. The City of New Haven provided use of the records of the Board of Aldermen and correspondence and documents relating to City ownership of the New Haven Water Company.

We intend this bibliography to serve as a convenience for readers, future researchers, and those who wish to use this book as a real world model demonstrating how a regional water utility came to be and how it has conserved open space while providing safe and affordable drinking water to consumers.

Abbreviations

In citing works in the bibliography the following abbreviations have been used:

NHWC	New Haven Water Company
SCCRWA	South Central Connecticut Regional Water Authority
FSC	Commission to Study the Feasibility of a South Central Connecticut Regional Water District
PA	Public Act
SA	Special Act
HB (or SB)	House (or Senate) bill
sHB (or sSB)	Substitute House (or Senate) bill
RAE	General Assembly Regulated Activities and Energy Committee

ENV   General Assembly Environment Committee
Conn.   Connecticut

An Act Incorporating the NHWC. Resolves and Private Laws of the
    State of Conn. (1836-1856), 4:1369.

Bai, Matt et al. "Does New York Have A Drinking Problem?" *New
    York*, 16 January 1995: 25-31.

Beck, R. W. and Associates. *Summary of Engineering Report on
    Acquisition of Water Utility Properties on NHWC by City of
    New Haven, Conn.* Wellesley, 1 November 1977.

——. *Engineering Report: Comprehensive Technical Evaluations
    of the NHWC Facilities.* Wellesley, January 1980.

——. *Update of Comparison of Estimated Annual Revenue
    Requirements.* Wellesley, 23 May 1980.

Black, Hallie. "Connecticut puts a damper on Water Company land
    sales." *Planning.* American Society of Planning Officials,
    January 1977.

Bridgeport Hydraulic Company v. Council on Water Company
    Lands, 453 Supp. 942 (D. Conn. 1977) aff'd 439 U. S. 999
    (1978).

Brooks, Howard D. Remarks to the RPB. 16 January 1992.

——. Memo to Representative McCluskey. 22 July 1977.

Cahn Engineering. "Pre-Study of the NHWC Watershed Lands."
    1974.

Carbonell, A. J. "Approaches to Protecting Connecticut's Water
    Utility Lands." Conn. Department of Environmental
    Protection, January 1975.

City of New Haven Board of Aldermen. *Resolution of the City of New
    Haven Authorizing the Mayor to Submit an Offer to Purchase
    the NHWC and Order Pursuant Thereto.* Public hearing. 8
    December 1977.

——. *Minutes.* 8 December 1977, 14 April 1978, 26 June 1978.

Cohen, Matthew. *Regulating the Use of Water Company Land:A
    Strategy for Connecticut Lawmakers.* Report to Conn.
    General Assembly Water Company Lands Subcommittee.
    Yale Legislative Services, October 1977.

Conn. Council on Environmental Quality. "Disposition of Water-shed Lands." 1974.

Conn. Department of Environmental Protection. *Conn. Statewide Comprehensive Recreation Plan.* 1973.

Conn. Department of Health. *Analysis of Connecticut's Public Water Supplies.* 1966-70

Conn. Gen. Assembly. Office of Legislative Research. *Bonding for Water* Companies. 23 October 1974.

——. *An Act Concerning the SCCRWA. Summary of the Bill.* 3 April 1978.

——. *Water Company Lands: Summary of Council Report.* 9 March 1977.

——. *Report of the Connecticut Council on Water Company Lands.* February 1977.

——. *Report of the Commission to Study the Feasibility of a South Central Connecticut Regional Water District.* 5 January 1977.

——. HB 7669 *An Act Concerning the Sale of Water Company Lands.*

——. SB 504, subsequently sHB5691, *An Act Authorizing the City of New Haven to Purchase or Condemn the NHWC and Operate a Regional Water System,* 1976

——. HB 5995 *An Act Establishing a SCCRWA,* 1977.

——. HB 7958, as amended by LCO 8874, *An Act Concerning Financial Assistance for Water Companies for Construction of Treatment Facilities.*

——. *20 House of Representatives Proceedings,* Pt. 16, 1977: 6535-6568.

——. *Special Session,* Pt. 10, 1977: 4296-4317.

——. *Special Session,* Pt. 16, 1977: 6923-6949.

——. *20 Senate Proceedings,* Pt. 10, 1977: 4119-4222.

Conn. Joint Standing Committee Hearings, ENV. Pt. 1, 18 March 1975.

——. ENV. Pt. 4, 10 and 18 March 1997.

——. RAE. Pt. 1, 25 March 1976.

——. RAE. Pt. 14, 14 February 1977.

——. RAE/ENV. Pt. 1, 26 February 1977.

Conn. Office of Policy and Management. Secretary Anthony V. Milano Memo to Gov. Ella T. Grasso and the General Assembly. "Safe Drinking Water - Economic Impact Analysis". 26 March 1979.

Conn. Office of State Planning. Dept. of Finance and Control. *Proposed: A Plan of Conservation and Development for Connecticut.* January 1973.

Conn. Public Acts. 75130 *An Act Concerning the State Plan of Conservation and Development.*

——. 75-405 *An Act Concerning the Sale of Water Company Lands.*

——. 77-606 *An Act Concerning the Council on Water Company Lands.*

Conn. Special Acts. 77-98 *An Act Concerning Financial Assistance for Water Companies for Construction of Treatment Facilities and Creating a SCCRWA.*

Conn. Public Acts. 78-24 *An Act Concerning the SCCRWA.*

Cooper, Peter B. *The Woodbridge Report: The Town's Potential Role in Acquiring Partial Interests and Rights in NHWC Land.* Prepared for the Regional Committee on NHWC Land Study. Regional Planning Agency, 6 February 1975.

Corbin, Arthur. *History of the NHWC.* SCCRWA. 1954 (mimeo graphed).

Crawford, John. Letter to Bennitt. 17 October 1994.

Curran, Ward S. *Rate of Return of Stockholders Investment in NHWC 1974-1976.* Mimeographed.

Daniels, John. Letter to the Board of Aldermen. 8 November 1977.

Ebasco Services Incorporated. *Preliminary Report on Proposed Acquisition of NHWC by the SCCRWA.* December 1977.

FSC Report, Public hearings. 12 October 1976, 14 October 1976.

Gallagher, Robert, First Vice President Bache Halsey Stuart, Inc. Letter to Vincent Mascia. 1976.

Greenwich water company, et al. v. Howard E. Hausman, (J.D. Hartford/New Britain, Docket No 10838, May 12, 1979) cert. denied, 178 Conn. 755 (1979).

Grasso, Governor Ella T. Letter to Senator James J. Murphy, Jr. and Representative John W. Anderson. 8 March 1977.

Houlding, Andrew L. Five-part series of articles. *Journal-Courier.* 3-

7 April 1978.

Household Hazardous Waste Collection Center, *Fiscal Year Budget*, 1995.

Irland, Lloyd C. and Stephen Levy. "Municipal Watershed Use Conflicts in Southern New England." Working paper. Institution for Social and Policy Studies, Yale University, January 1975.

Jackson, Jay W. Memo to Governor Ella T. Grasso. 19 July 1977.

Joint discussion. "The New England Water Utility Story." *Journal of the American Waterworks Association.* vol. 66, No.4. April 1974.

Logue, Mayor Frank. Letter to Board of Aldermen of the City of New Haven. 8 Nov. 1977.

——. Testimony to Board of Aldermen. 8 December 1977.

Lufkin, Dan W. "Response: Utility Company Lands." *Connecticut Woodlands.* vol. 39 no. 1 (Spring 1974): 10, 11, 19.

Madden, Senator B. Patrick. Letter to Governor Ella T. Grasso. 19 July 1977.

McCluskey, Representative Dorothy S. Letter to North Branford Town Council regarding FSC report and recommendations. 1 February 1977.

——. Letter to Governor Ella T. Grasso. 19 July 1977.

——. and Representative Gerald F. Stevens and Senator Madden. Memo to Members of the General Assembly. 20 July 1977.

McHugh, Richard and Otto Schaefer. Correspondence and Memo on sale of Wintergreen land. 1983.

Morgan Guaranty Trust Company of New York. *Several Applications for Evaluation of the NHWC.* New York, 15 December 1977.

NHWC. *Annual Reports.* 1968-1979.

——. Board of Directors. *Minutes.* 1970-1980.

——. Charles E. Woods' Letter to Stockholders. 30 March 1978.

Newspapers:

Bridgeport Telegram. 21 May 1975.

Branford Review. 19 December 1974, 30 January 1975, 1 April 1976, 6 May 1976.

Christian Science Monitor. 11 April 1977.

Hartford Courant. 12 January 1974, 5 July 1975, 28 February 1977, 5 January 1979, 20 April 1979.

Meriden Morning Record (The Morning Record in 1975). 17 October 1974, 8 July 1975, 18 March 1976, 2 April 1977, 16 July 1977.

Journal-Courier. 24 September 1974, 8 April 1977, 7 June 1977, 8 June 1977, 3-8 April 1978, 24 June 1981.

New Haven Register. 13 April 1966, 3 April 1973, 13 July 1973, 2 January 1974, 26 April 1974, 12 October 1975, 8 March 1976, 1 April 1976, 6 April 1976, 12 March 1976, 28 March 1976, 30 March 1976, 26 September 1976, 5 February 1977, 18 February 1977 editorial, 13 March 1977 editorial, 15 July 1977 editorial, 17 July 1977, 9 November 1977, 28 January 1978, 28 April 1978, 21 December 1978, 10 April 1978 editorial, 5 January 1979, 9 January 1979, 22 February 1979, 20 April 1979, 17 May 1980, 28 June 1981.

New York Times. 1 May 1977, 23 March 1994, 12 December 1994 editorial, 15 May 1994 editorial, 28 May 1994 letter in response to editorial, 16 January 1995 editorial, 26 April 1995, 29 September 1995 editorial.

The Advertiser. 4 April 1977, 18 April 1977, 13 June 1977, 7 December 1977, 23 April 1979.

The Wallingford Post. 27 February 1975.

Okun, Daniel A. "Best Available Source". *Journal of the American Waterworks Association*, 83:3:30, March 1991.

Olmstead, Frederick Law, Jr., and Gilbert Cass. *New Haven Civic Improvement Commission Report.* New Haven: Tuttle, Morehouse and Taylor, 1910.

Oscherwitz, Jan C. "The History of the NHWC: Redefining Public Need." Senior Essay, Yale University, 23 April 1984. (mimeographed)

Regulations of Conn. State Agencies. Dept. of Health Water Company Land Classification. Sec. 25-37c-1 through 25-32d-10 (1980).

Report of the Special Committee on Water of the Court of Common

Council. *Contract Between the City of New Haven and the NHWC.* 17 February 1902.

Richards, Sarah W. "Conn. Council on Water Company Lands address to the Yale School of Forestry and Environmental Studies Workshop". 30 March 1977.

Rogers, Judith Lee. "New Haven Water". SCCRWA 1983 (mimeographed).

Rogers, Peter. *America's Water: Federal Roles and Responsibilities.* A Twentieth Century Fund Book, 1993.

Safe Drinking Water Act, 42 U. S. C. 300 et seq. (1974).

SCCRWA. *Acquisition Plan.* 28 December 1980-1993.

——. *Agreement and Plan of Merger of NHWC.* 6 March 1980.

——. *Annual Reports.* 1980-1993

——. *General Bond Resolution.* 31 July 1980.

——. *Minutes.* 8 and 11 December 1977, 11 January 1978, 12 February 1978, 7 March 1978, 30 November 1978, 3 July 1979, 5 October 1979, 12 December 1989, 5 April 1980, 1 October 1980.

——. Lake Saltonstall Native Trail *Guide.*

——. *New Haven Board of Aldermen Agreement.* 21 June 1978.

——. *Land Use Plan* 1983.

——. *Land Use Plan* 1993 Update.

——. *Land Use Plan* 1995 Update.

Official Statement. Special Obligation Bonds, First Series. 1 August 1980.

——. *Official Statement.* 8 August 1980.

Official Statement. Water System Revenue Bonds, First Series. 1 August 1980.

Snyder, William. Report to Joel Cohn. *Feasibility Study of Reorganization of NHWC into Municipally Owned Utility.* 1975.

Stave, Krystyna A. "Resource Conflict in New York City's Catskill Watersheds: A Case for Expanding the Scope of Water Resource Management." American Water Resources Association conference presentation. April 1995: 3.

Stern, Peter M. "Utility Company Lands." *Connecticut Woodlands.* vol. 39, no. 1 (Spring 1974): 6, 7.

Strong, Ann Louise (ed.). *Open Space Through Water Resources Protection*. Philadelphia: Institute for Environmental Studies, University of Pennsylvania, 1965.

U. S. Council on Environmental Quality. *Recreation on Water Supply Reservoirs: A Handbook for Increased Use*. September 1975.

Wilkinson, Richard R. et al. *The Integration of Multiple Objectives in Urbanizing Watersheds*. Water Resources Research Institute, University of North Carolina, 1972.

The Newark Watershed Conservation and Development Corporation. *The Pequannock Watershed Conservation and Development Plan*. Report to Mayor K.A. Gibson. June 1975.

The Trust for Public Land. *Green Cities Initiative: Healing America's Cities*. 1994-1995. Boston.

——."Watershed Protection Has Mainstream Appeal". *Green Sense: Financing Parts and Conservation,* vol. 2 no. 1. Spring 1996

"Town Develops Aquifer Protection Regulations." *American City and Country*, February 1995: 56.

Wexler, Harry J. Memo *to* FSC. 17 June 1977.

Woodhull, Richard S. "Connecticut's Safe Water Drinking Act." 1975.

——. *Implementation of 77-606: Report to Legislative Subcommittee on Water Company Lands*. 7 December 1978.

——. Letter to Charles E., Woods 13 September 1979.

Woods, Charles E., Letter to All Management Employees. "Statement, Re: NHWC's Plans for Formation of a Holding Company." 27 November 1972.

——. Letter to candidate McCluskey. 25 September 1974.

——. Letters to Harry J. Wexler. 8 April 1976 and 9 September 1976.

——. Letter to Howard D. Brooks. 18 October 1977.

——. Memo to file. 27 September 1979.

——. "Utility Company Lands." *Connecticut Woodlands*. vol. 23, no. 1 (Spring 1974): 7-9.

Williams,, Edward P. "Water Utility Land Use." *Connecticut Woodlands*. vol. 23, no. 1 (Spring 1974): 4-6.

Yale Task Force on Water Company Lands, School of Forestry and Environmental Studies. *Connecticut's Water Supply Lands:*

Information on Selected Utilities. Information booklet for public forum. New Haven: Environment Education Center, December 1976.